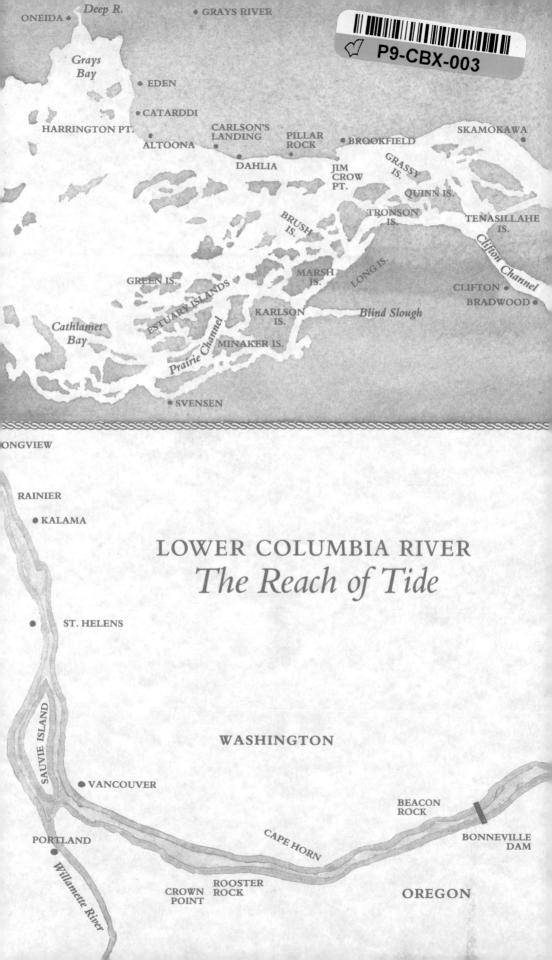

ONEIDA •   *Deep R.*   • GRAYS RIVER

Grays Bay

• EDEN

• CATARDDI

HARRINGTON PT. •

ALTOONA •

CARLSON'S LANDING

PILLAR ROCK

• BROOKFIELD

SKAMOKAWA •

DAHLIA •

JIM CROW PT.

GRASSY IS.

QUINN IS.

TRONSON IS.

TENASILLAHE IS.

BRUSH IS.

GREEN IS.

MARSH IS.

LONG IS.

Clifton Channel

ESTUARY ISLANDS

KARLSON IS.

Blind Slough

CLIFTON •

BRADWOOD •

Cathlamet Bay

Prairie Channel

MINAKER IS.

• SVENSEN

ONGVIEW

RAINIER

• KALAMA

LOWER COLUMBIA RIVER
The Reach of Tide

• ST. HELENS

SAUVIE ISLAND

WASHINGTON

• VANCOUVER

BEACON ROCK

PORTLAND •

CAPE HORN

BONNEVILLE DAM

Willamette River

CROWN POINT

ROOSTER ROCK

OREGON

Reach of Tide / Ring of History

COLUMBIA RIVER HERITAGE SERIES

Reach of Tide

Illustrations by Elsa Warnick

1987

Ring of History

A COLUMBIA RIVER VOYAGE

SAM McKINNEY

Sam McKinney (signature)

OREGON HISTORICAL SOCIETY PRESS

THE ENDPAPER MAP illustrates the Columbia River from
its mouth at the Pacific Ocean to the Bonneville Dam, the "reach of tide."
The two insets show sections of the river in greater detail.
(Maps by Rachael R. Resch)

The author wishes to express his thanks to Steve Lee of the Stash Tea Company,
whose support made this voyage possible.

Library of Congress Cataloging in Publication Data
McKinney, Sam, 1927–
  Reach of tide, ring of history.

  Bibliography: p.
  Includes index.
  1. Columbia River—Description and travel.
2. Columbia River Valley—History.   3. McKinney, Sam,
1927–   . Journeys—Columbia River.
4. Sailing—Columbia River.   I. Title.
F853.M34   1987   917.97'0443   87-13904
ISBN 0-87595-196-1

The paper used in this publication meets the minimum requirements of American
National Standard for Information Sciences—Permanence of Paper for Printed Library
Materials, ANSI Z39.48-1984.

This volume was designed and produced by the Oregon Historical Society Press.

Printed in the United States of America.

*Dedicated to the memory
of my* UNCLE IVAN.
*When I was a boy,
he gave me a boat and oars,
and sent me on my way.*

Contents

Preface

As the voyage by boat up the Columbia was a journey, so, too, was the writing of this book. It was a journey into my own past by which I discovered those places and events along the Columbia River that largely shaped my life. The voyage and writing the book together were, for me, what French author and philosopher Albert Camus calls that "trek to rediscover, through the detours of art, those two or three great and simple images in whose presence our heart first opened."

I call these images the sources of spirit. The indigenous people of the river shores saw the Columbia as a place of spirit. In less conscious ways, so do the people I write about in this book perceive the river.

My book borders on the edge of nostalgia given the dignity of history. But I hope that what I have written will reveal that the Columbia is more than a river of nostalgia and history. For our time (and never before so needed) it is a place, a presence, a force, and a source for spiritual replenishment. I would urge you to discover, through whatever your art, this river, this life source of our lives.

Reach of Tide / Ring of History

Bearings

My boat lifted and fell in the gentle ocean swell a few miles seaward from Cape Disappointment off the mouth of the Columbia River. Although the summer morning was calm, my exposed offshore position made me nervous. I was in a small boat I had built for a journey up the Columbia, not for a voyage on the open ocean. But the journey had to begin from the sea if I was to approach the river, cross its bar, and then travel upstream as a sailing ship had done nearly two centuries ago to begin the first chapter of the river's recorded history.

Going to sea in a small boat was the first of many difficulties I was prepared to endure to attain the objective of my journey – a personal exploration of the tidal reach of the Columbia along the shoreline of its maritime history. Exposure to wind, wave, rain, and sun with its attendant discomforts was the price I was prepared to pay in order to personally experience the climate, the conditions, and the moods of the river which had shaped history and the lives of the people who have lived and worked along its shores.

The fading current of an ebbing tide had carried me through the buoyed ship channel and out past the broken ends of the two stone jetties which define the outer ramparts of the river mouth. Sea birds floating on the easy swells of their restless roosts skittered before me and then resettled on the sea in clusters to preen themselves as they bobbed up and down on the ocean waves. The deep-sea sound of a distant bell buoy gave to the morning a mood of space and timelessness as the gong clanged to the slow roll of the long Pacific swells. Except for the birds, I was alone on the sea.

Turning the boat, I looked back at the coast. To the north, the descending spine of Cape Disappointment ended in a steep cliff. To the south, the low sands of Clatsop Spit formed the blur of a distant beach. To my eyes, these two points appeared to be united by the backdrop of dark Washington hills which seemed to tie the land together in one long, unbroken shore between Tillamook Head to the south, and the diminishing line of the Long Beach Peninsula to the north. Were it not for the jetties and the line of the buoys, I would have lost sight of the river entrance.

I tried to picture the Columbia as it must have appeared to an eighteenth-century maritime explorer, when sandbars filled the river mouth. I could imagine his view: Swells, breaking on those bars, would have appeared to him as a continuation of

the surf which broke north and south of the river in an uninter-
rupted white line. The view gained by my short sea voyage explained to me why the Columbia was the last of the world's great
rivers to be discovered. To that eighteenth-century ship captain,
the Columbia River was nearly invisible.

Though unseen, it had a name: The River of the West. It
was a river that had to exist because the logic of geographical
thought said it existed and because imagination – fired by the
ambitions of political and economic power – wanted it to. The
search for the River of the West was a continuum in the efforts of
humans throughout history to find in reality that which is projected by desire and imagination.

What was hoped for was a commercial waterway that
would cross North America. A geographical theory at that time
supported the existence of such a waterway. The theory held
that from a collective height of land somewhere on the continent
there fell four rivers; one for each cardinal point of the compass.
There was the River of the East (the St. Lawrence), the River
of the South (the Mississippi) and evidence of the River of the
North. The missing link was the River of the West. If it could be
found, the seas washing the continent would be linked by an
interior waterway.

The Columbia was first noted by Spanish captain Bruno
de Hezeta as he was returning in his ship *Santiago* from an ex-
ploring voyage north along the coast in 1775. With his crew reduced by illness and death, Hezeta was unable to investigate the
suspected river.

Three names he left behind. The prominent cape on the
north side of the river entrance (Cape Disappointment) he called
Cabo San Roque. On the south side, Hezeta named present-day
Point Adams, which was then apparently tree-covered, *Cabo
Frondoso*. The bay between was named *Bahia de la Asunción* in
honor of the feast day on which it was discovered. Hezeta never
actually entered the river itself, although the strong currents he
experienced at the mouth of the bay convinced him that such a
river existed. He wrote on 17 August 1775: "These currents and

the seething of the waters have led me to believe that it may be the mouth of some great river or some passage to another sea." Spanish cartographers called this probable river *Rio San Roque*, and included it on their coastal maps.

English captain James Cook passed by the river on his northward passage along the coast in 1776. John Meares, an independent trader, was sailing south along the coast in 1788 when he found himself off the location of the reported Rio San Roque. Unable to see the river, he declared it did not exist. His disappointment in not finding the river – and the trading opportunities it might have offered – was expressed by the names he left behind to replace the Spanish names. Cabo San Roque he called Cape Disappointment and Bahia de la Asunción he renamed Deception Bay.

One more great navigator and explorer was to sail past the river without seeing it. George Vancouver had sailed as an officer with Cook. He returned to the coast in his own ship *Discovery* with instructions to complete Cook's survey of the Northwest Coast.

On 27 April 1792, Vancouver identified Meares' Deception Bay, which he described this way:

On the south side of this promontory [Cape Disappointment] *was the appearance of an inlet, or small river, the land not indicating it to be of any great extent; nor did it seem accessible for vessels of our burthen, as the breakers extended from the above point two or three miles into the ocean, until they joined those on the beach nearly four leagues further south.*

What I saw during my short voyage on the sea confirmed the description Vancouver wrote two centuries ago describing the river mouth. All he noted was a change in the color of the seawater which he attributed to:

the probable consequence of some streams falling into the bay, or into the ocean to the north of it, through the low land. Not considering this opening

*worthy of more attention, I continued our pursuit to the N.W. being
desirous to embrace the advantages of the prevailing breeze.*

Vancouver sailed on and the Columbia remained hidden.

The water around my boat began to stir, and flow lines
around the base of the buoy indicated a change to a flooding tide.
I looked at my watch. The time was right; 8:00 A.M. And then
I checked the compass. Course: East-north-east. I turned and
headed for the river entrance hoping to cross the bar as closely as
I could to the time and course of the ship that first entered the
Columbia River.

Robert Gray was an American free trader. Under his
command, the ship *Columbia Rediviva* was the first American ship
to make a round-the-world voyage. In 1792, Gray was on his
second trading voyage to the Northwest Coast. His practice was
to sail close along the shore seeking out small bays and openings
that might shelter natives willing to trade. It was a practical Yan-
kee desire for trade and profit, not fame for exploration and discovery, that prompted him to hazard the crossing of the shallow
bar of an unknown inlet on the morning of 11 May 1792. The tide
was just right, the wind was in the right quarter and the sea was
calm. Because of these chance conditions, the Columbia River
entered history with this brief log entry:

*At eight, a.m., being a little to windward of the entrance of the Harbor,
bore away, and ran in east-north-east between the breakers, having from
five to seven fathoms of water. When we were over the bar, we found this
to be a large river of fresh water, up which we steered.*

I followed, crossed the bar, and up the river I steered.
I had started my voyage at the beginning of the river and its
history.

The bar of the Columbia River

CROSSING THE BAR on a calm sea with a push from a strong
flooding current was, for me, an exhilarating way to enter the
Columbia River. For other vessels, the same short journey has
ended in disaster. Since Gray first crossed the bar, it has claimed
over two thousand boats and ships, and at least fifteen hundred
lives.

Alexander Ross, who crossed the bar on the ship *Tonquin* in 1811 with the loss of eight men, described the natural condition of the bar.

The bar, or rather the chain of sand banks, over which the huge waves and foaming breakers roll so awfully, is a league broad, and extends in a white foaming sheet for many miles, both south and north of the mouth of the river, forming as it were an impracticable barrier to the entrance, and threatening with instant destruction everything that comes near it.

A century of marine engineering at the mouth of the Columbia has removed the chain of sandbanks that Ross encountered. Even so, the bar of the Columbia still holds a reputation as a maritime terror.

As a place, it is invisible to the eye. It exists as a fragile but permanent underwater front that stands between river and ocean, an accumulation of water-washed sand. To the mariner, a bar is a natural condition to be expected and anticipated at the mouth of any river. It is comprehensible if perceived as a result of the conflict of opposing energies and substances seeking equilibrium in the timeless encounter of forces which meet when a river runs into the sea.

The river I entered as I crossed over the bar carries the accumulated waters of a five-state, two-nation region. The quarter-million square-mile watershed area of the Columbia is bordered along the west by the Coast Range and on the east by the Continental Divide. It contains the major land areas of Oregon, Washington, and Idaho, western Montana, the northwestern corner of Wyoming and southwestern British Columbia. The water flow of the full river is double the volume of the Missouri and ten times greater than the Colorado. It is the largest river flowing into the ocean along the entire Pacific Coast of North and South America. All of this water returns to the sea through the narrow jaws of the river mouth.

That five-state, two-nation watershed of the Columbia is a region of mountains. To get to the sea, the river has to carve its channel through these mountains by grinding rock into sand. Its currents then sluice the channel they carve and carry the sands downstream to where they are deposited at the mouth of the river. The process has been going on for millions of years. The river is still carving its way to the sea. Sand continues to accumulate at the mouth of the river.

Ocean currents and wave action work to carry away the deposits. The long sandy beaches of Oregon and southern Washington are evidence of the sea-carried river sands which pile to form this coast. But the river delivers more sand than the ocean can carry away. The surplus accumulates at the river mouth to form the place called "The Bar."

This process is slow, gentle and constant. Not so is the edge of the sea, a place of violent wind and wave. Both come driving in from thousands of miles of unrestrained travel across the open Pacific. When the wave confronts the shoal created by the steep, abrupt seaward side of the bar, its forward speed at the base decreases, its height increases and the distance between each wave crest shortens. The tumbling energy of the wave concentrates in the lifting menace of its crest. Higher and higher it grows until its unstable shape can no longer support its own weight and it collapses in a welter of released power that breaks and plunges over its advancing front.

Conditions on the bar can be even worse if an ebbing tide meets incoming winds, which tear at the surface of the outgoing current, creating huge waves. Four times in each twenty-four-hour period the tide moves in and out of the river. As the incoming tide advances up the Columbia, the flood of intruding water creates a dam that blocks and reverses the river current. When the tide runs out, the combined waters of the flood tide and the impounded river return to the sea in a rushing wash of force. It is this condition of a fast ebbing current in collision with the incoming wave and wind that creates the dreaded conditions of the Columbia River bar. The collected horror stories of the vessels caught in this situation are the bar's legends of shipwreck, disaster and death.

Controlling the forces that are concentrated at the bar defies any human effort. But by working with these forces instead of opposing them, engineering has partially tamed the river's entrance to make it safe for vessels. The key was to build structures that encouraged rather than restricted the passage of current and wave. The two stone jetties projecting seaward from the mouth of the Columbia and the dredged channel lying between them serve this purpose.

Just inside of the river mouth, I turned out of the channel and beached my boat in the protected shallows behind Clatsop Spit. From there, it was a short walk over the sand to reach the south jetty, an unbroken wall of rough, unmortared rocks that extends seaward for four miles. Along the flat line of its ridge lay the broken and weathered ruins of the old railway track that was used to construct the jetty. Stepping carefully over timbers and stones, I walked along the top of the jetty on a narrow line that separated breaking ocean waves on my left from a quietly running river on my right. That wall and its counterpart, the north jetty on the Washington shore, are the controlling structures in the engineered system that maintains a channel for the safe passage of ships over the Columbia River bar.

Though the jetties are static, the process of channel maintenance they create is dynamic. The twin jetties direct the natural forces of river and tidal currents into a concentrated zone of current that is strong enough to sluice its own channel. They do not, like a seawall, enclose an area of sheltered water.

The collective projects of jetty construction, channel dredging and the placement of navigation aids at the mouth of the Columbia rank as one of the world's most impressive feats of marine engineering. It began with the first attempt to survey the river in 1839 by Sir Edward Belcher. His soundings showed that the natural conditions of the river created two channels. One channel led close under the foot of Cape Disappointment, and a second or southern channel was just offshore of Point Adams. The two channels were separated by the wide shallow areas of the Middle Bank and the low rise of Sand Island.

The first American survey of the river was made in 1841 by a U.S. Navy expedition under command of Lieutenant Charles Wilkes. One of his survey ships, the *Peacock*, grounded on the shoal below Cape Disappointment to leave both its bones and its name on this infamous spit. In 1850, Lieutenant Commander William McArthur completed an examination of the river for the U.S. Coast Survey. His survey revealed that neither of the two channels were deep enough or dependable enough to provide safe entry to or exit from the river mouth.

In 1882, the U.S. Army Corps of Engineers submitted a plan for the construction of an eight thousand–foot-long jetty that would extend seaward from Fort Stevens on the south cape. Cost was estimated at $3,710,000. Work on the jetty began in 1884 and took ten years to complete.

The construction of the jetty involved three steps. Initially, a double track was built above and ahead of the projected crest of the jetty. A steam engine and thirty flatcars operated on this track. Next, the foundations of the jetty were placed. These consisted of iron pilings driven into the sand, followed by the placement of wired mattresses of brush and small rocks to minimize erosion under the stonework of the jetty. Stone was then barged to the jetty location, placed aboard the flatcars, hauled to the edge of the jetty and dumped. When completed in 1895, the south jetty created a channel through the bar with a minimum depth of thirty feet.

Surveys within only two years, however, showed that the channel was again shoaling. In 1902, approval was given to improve the existing four-mile jetty and to extend it for another three miles. Rough seas caused extensive damage to the wooden train trestle during the winter storms of 1905-1906, and over five miles of track were destroyed. By 1913, the project was completed at a cost of nearly $4 million. It created thirty-seven feet of safe water over the bar. A decision was then made to construct a north jetty in hopes of obtaining a channel depth of forty feet. Work on the north jetty began in 1914 and was completed in 1917 at an additional cost of $6 million. When the two jetties at the mouth of the river were completed, they were the largest in the world.

After World War II, ship size increased, particularly the draft of tanker ships, and drafts of more than thirty feet were becoming common. A thirty-foot draft over a forty-foot bottom does not provide a ship with an adequate safety margin. In rough water, a ship pitches fore and aft in a movement known as "sounding." This motion can add fifteen feet to a vessel's draft at bow and stern, and ships were forced to cross the bar with less than load capacities in order to decrease draft and maintain safety margins. Since the sluicing action of the two jetties alone did not create the necessary forty-eight-foot depth, dredges were put to work on the river in 1956 to deepen the channel. Over seventeen million yards of sand were removed by the dredges to gain the desired channel depth. Periodic dredging is still necessary to keep the channel open.

I walked out as far as I could along the jetty and then sat down behind the protection of a rock to just look at the dramatic junction of the river and the ocean. It is a place that few people have ever visited and yet the livelihoods of many who live within the reach of the Columbia River depend, ultimately, on the two low, sullen stonewalls that together enable the river to wash away the sands that otherwise would clog its mouth. Without them, the inland ports of the Columbia would be river towns without access to the sea. Because of them, the cities of the river region have an open water route across the river bar to the world.

Pilots across the bar

A DAY LATER I crossed the bar again, not in my own boat, but as a passenger aboard the bar pilot boat *Columbia*. It had taken a considerable amount of letter writing and a number of telephone calls before I was given permission from the no-nonsense Columbia River Bar Pilots Association to ride out aboard a pilot ship.

I approached the association's office, which is housed on the Astoria waterfront, with a sense of reverence, remembering my first encounter with the bar and a bar pilot during World War II when I was a seventeen-year-old quartermaster on a wartime Liberty ship. From out of a black night the pilot had come by small boat to take charge of the darkened ship as it headed for an outward-bound, winter crossing of the bar. I cursed the luck that had brought me seasick, inexperienced and frightened to the bridge after midnight, during the first watch that would see the ship heading to sea. The only light on the bridge was the weak glimmer of the compass card that stood in front of my position behind the wheel. All channel markers had been removed from the river as a wartime security measure.

Outside, the shuddering encounter with the first large wave breaking on the bar dropped the deck from under me. With a sense of near panic, I waited for the next wave to come crashing through the windows of the wheelhouse and engulf the ship. The pilot, an unseen presence in the darkness of the bridge, calmly spoke to me. "Steady on two-four-zero," came his reassuring voice, and all fear left me as I concentrated on holding the ship's course in line with the points of the compass card. "Come left to two-two-five," he ordered, and I felt a sense of thrill as I swung the wheel and held the ship on its new heading. The pilot – with his mystical vision and sense of time, distance and location – was my eyes. I was his hands. Together we commanded a ship; his skill and his voice, my ears and my hands. Responding to each other, they carried us through the black night and across the bar to the safety of the open sea.

He was but one in a legendary line of men who have banded together in the Columbia River Bar Pilots Association to offer, for a fee, their services as pilots to ships entering and clearing the mouth of the Columbia River. These pilots limit their services to bar passages and they do not guide ships up and down the river above Astoria. Each pilot owns a share of the jointly held corporation. There are no outside owners or investors. If a member retires or quits, his share is purchased by the corporation and resold to a new member.

The average age of the pilots is well over forty. For a period of eight weeks, a pilot works on a rotational basis that keeps him on call twenty-four hours a day, seven days a week. At the conclusion of the eight-week duty period, the pilot goes off call for the next four months. At full force, the association is composed of twenty-two pilot-members. Each pilot holds an unlimited master's license and has behind him a minimum of five years of command. If accepted as a member of the association, the apprentice pilot must make one hundred trips before he can qualify as a pilot. In addition, each man must also pass a rigorous Coast Guard examination.

Essentially, the association is a closed corporation not unlike a medieval guild in which entrance into a closed circle of professionals is controlled by those already within it. The pilots are united by the common bond of performing a mutual task that requires great skill and judgment. It is a job which confronts them equally with the hazards of one of the world's most dangerous river bars. The pilots have earned the right to be exclusive; their common reputation is no better than the least of them.

Old Chief Comcomly, the Chinook Indian chief at the time of the founding of the Astor colony, was the first officially recognized bar pilot. From his lookout on Scarborough Hill behind Chinook Point, the old chief had an unobstructed view of the river mouth. Sighting a ship, Comcomly would be paddled out in his canoe to meet the ship and assist it over the bar. His knowledge of the channel was accurate enough for him to be acknowledged as the chief pilot for the Hudson's Bay Company.

During the first half of the nineteenth century, a bar pilot was anyone who so qualified himself. Numerous shipwrecks during that time were due to pilot ignorance or negligence. In 1846, the Oregon legislature established license requirements for pilots, and the first license was issued to Captain S.C. Reeves. He put three ships on the sands at the mouth of the river entrance before returning to San Francisco where he drowned in 1849 when a squall overturned his sloop in the bay.

On Christmas Day, 1849, the sixty-foot *Mary Taylor*, under the command of Captain Jackson Hustler, arrived in Astoria. Hustler, along with Cornelius John White and Captain John Whitefield, operated the *Mary Taylor* for the next three years as a pilot boat. Another early pilot boat was a sloop-rigged launch saved from the wreck of the *Peacock*. This boat was operated by George Gear and Robert Alexander. At best, the services offered by these early pilots were haphazard and unreliable. Ships sometimes had to lay off the mouth of the Columbia for days waiting for weather conditions that would permit the pilot boats to come out.

In 1850, Captain George Flavel placed his schooner *California* in service on the bar, and through shrewd management and superior service he was able to maintain a near monopoly over pilot services for the next decade. Flavel was born in Norfolk, Virginia, in 1823, and became a shipmaster at a very young age. One of his first commands took him to the West Coast where he settled in Astoria and created a shipping empire at the mouth of the Columbia River. The ornate Victorian mansion he built in Astoria at the corner of Eighth and Duane streets is now the home of the Clatsop County Historical Society.

An attempt to break Flavel's monopoly was made in 1865 by Captain Paul Corno with his steam tug *Rabboni*. The *Rabboni* was the first steam tug to operate on the bar. Even with his new tug, Corno could not compete with the reputation and efficiency of Flavel and he, too, returned to San Francisco.

Tug assistance over the bar, however, was considered essential to safety, and a subsidy of $30,000 was offered by the Oregon legislature to anyone who could operate a tug on the river for five continuous years. Flavel built the steam tug *Astoria*, which he operated for the required length of time to collect the full subsidy.

On the day that I walked into the pilot office, I was introduced to eighty-year-old Tom Clark. Tom, who greeted me with his sleeves rolled up, a pipe in his mouth and a green sunshade over his eyes, is the radio and telephone voice for the pilot service. He has been interviewed many times and knows all the questions before they are asked. Perhaps because he wanted to avoid one more boring interview, he fired off the first question as I sat down across from him.

"Know what would happen if you crossed an elephant with a swimsuit?"

Taken aback by this irrelevancy in a place I considered almost sacred, I said I didn't know.

"Swimming trunks," he said and threw me a second riddle.

"Why is the Columbia River like a salmon?"

The shaking of my bewildered head communicated my ignorance as to why the Columbia River was like a salmon.

"Because it has Finns on both sides."

With those two quick one-liners, Tom told me that he is the author of a book containing 1500 jokes. I wondered if I was to hear the other 1,498 before beginning the interview. I mentioned the wonderful view of the river he had from his office window, hoping to lead him towards the question of how many ships he might have observed from that window during his long years with the association.

"Saw something besides ships," he informed me. "Two seagulls 'diddling' right there on that piling. Fellow took a picture of it and sold it for $1000."

Two seagulls "diddling" was obviously the most exciting thing Tom had ever seen from his window which frames the Columbia from Tongue Point to the Pacific, and includes the white line of Ilwaco on the distant Washington shore. I gave up my attempt to conduct an interview, put my notepad aside and just listened to Tom reminisce about his long career as a seagoing naval communications officer. After each anecdote, he would rummage in his desk drawer and bring out a news clipping, a letter or some other memento that served to illustrate his story.

"Know what is considered fast in sending and receiving telegraphic messages?" he asked as he showed me a commemorative letter written to him in World War II by Admiral A.W. Radford, commander of the Pacific Fleet. Again, I could only shrug my shoulders as a sign of my helpless ignorance.

"Sixty words a minute is considered fast. I've done sixty-six words a minute for fifteen minutes. Without error. Know where the largest ocean wave was ever recorded?"

"Yes," I replied. "It was measured off the southeast coast of Africa by the U.S. Navy ship *Ramapo*." Proudly, I sat back in my chair, feeling that authority had met authority.

"Wrong." Again he dove into his desk drawer and pulled out a reprint from an article in the *Scientific American* printed in 1959.

"It was in the Pacific. In a typhoon. I measured the wave."

Sure enough. There it was on page six. The wave measured 112 feet high. The place was the Pacific Ocean, 1933. I took some consolation in having properly named the ship.

"Here is something that will interest you," Tom exclaimed. He opened a dog-eared record book for my inspection and told me that between 1954 and 1981 he dispatched 105,000 ships entering or leaving the river. His job is to record requests for pilots and schedule the daily duty list for the pilots. Shipmasters are supposed to contact the station twelve hours before their arrival off the river bar, but Tom also depends on various shipping publications for the schedule of arriving and departing ships.

"Look at the subscription price of this," he said, holding up a thick publication. Under the masthead in small print I noted the subscription price of $800. "But we get it free," he chuckled as he returned the book to its assigned place in the orderly clutter of his desk.

The phone rang, the teletype clacked and Tom instantly

concentrated on a reply to a ship captain calling for a pilot. The question I would like to have asked him was how many faceless voices he has spoken to in his sixty-plus years of marine communications work. But he had turned away from me. It was not impoliteness; another message had to be put through. The jokes were put aside. The interview was over. A ship needed a pilot, and I was to go along for the ride.

The pilot and I left the office and took a cab to the association's private dock at Point Adams just inside the mouth of the river. It is faster and cheaper to drive downriver in a cab than it is to bring the pilot boat upriver to Astoria. We got out of the cab, walked along a narrow walkway through a locking gate and stepped down to the rubber-mesh deck of the waiting pilot boat *Columbia*. The instant my foot touched the deck, the boat backed out into the river. Boat operator Andy Carlson introduced himself and invited me to the pilot house where he motioned me to one of the two postchairs standing behind the twin engine controls of the boat. By the time I had found a safe place for my camera, tape recorder and notebook, and adjusted myself to the chair, we were at the mouth of the river. The bar crossing was again a calm trip, and I enjoyed a sun-sparkled cruise over a blue sea. A line of red buoys took us to our waiting position near the electronic buoy that has replaced the old manned lightship, also named *Columbia*.

"I miss that ship," said Andy. "When we were out here at night in winter, it was nice to know that we were not alone." The new electronic station does everything the old manned ship did except offer a sense of human companionship, which during a stormy winter night, kept the crew of the pilot boat from feeling that they were the only souls at sea.

At the end of his watch, Andy went below to cook a steak lunch, and was replaced at the wheel by Ken Olson. The cargo vessel we were to meet had emerged from the horizon and Ken moved the *Columbia* slowly ahead to intercept it. As we came up to it, the ship slowed to a speed of nearly five knots and turned crosswise in the wind to make a lee for the pilot boat to come up under.

A long rope ladder with wooden steps hung down from the freighter's side, its lower step dangling well above the surface of the sea. As the ship continued its slow forward movement, the *Columbia*'s course converged with it at an angle which just placed the bow of the pilot boat in touch with the side of the vessel and directly beneath the hanging ladder. Even though the ocean was calm, I was amazed at how much the pilot boat pitched and rolled as it closed with the looming side of the freighter. Under the ship's counter, the wash of the propellers and the break of the waves around the rudder revealed the tremendous power of the converging forces. Despite the turbulence, Ken maneuvered the *Columbia* forward to only an arm's distance from the towering side, into a controlled collision with the ship.

The pilot stepped onto the open foredeck of the pilot boat, grabbed a handrope and leaned out over the narrow angle of water rushing between boat and ship. Ken made a last critical maneuver and placed the pilot just beneath the suspended ladder on a course that held the boat nudged in against the side of the ship. At some instant judged only by the experience of having performed the act many times, the pilot let go of the handrope, leaped for the ladder, and, with its steps rattling beneath him, climbed the ship's side. The instant the pilot's foot left the boat, the *Columbia* moved out from under him and away from the ship, leaving only the surging sea beneath his climbing feet. No life jacket is worn by the pilot because it would restrict his movements. Whatever the condition, he gets one chance. It has to be the right one.

Under other conditions it is not so easy. As we waited to pick up a pilot from an outbound ship, the two boat operators showed me how the pilot is transferred during rough water conditions.

The afterdeck and transom of the *Columbia* form a wide V-shaped well that serves as the launching ramp for what is called the "daughter boat." It is a small, deep-bowed metal boat with the underbelly appearance of a whale. Ken sat at the controls of the boat, I sat in the passenger seat, and Andy released the launching cable which let the daughter boat slide down the stern ramp into the water. We hit the ocean with the engine running full speed in reverse for a fast scramble backwards and away from the stern of the *Columbia*. Using the *Columbia* as our incoming ship, Ken demonstrated how the daughter boat is used to place a pilot aboard a ship. The high-speed engine is coupled to a propeller by a clutch mechanism that allows the boat to be quickly shifted from full ahead speed to full reverse speed, making it possible to hold the boat in a precise position in the water. The ride over waves that tipped and bounced the boat up and down over the swells, sometimes hiding the *Columbia*, would have reminded me of a kid's boat ride at a carnival except that we were a tiny orange boat on the open sea.

Jumping from the broad deck of the *Columbia* to a rope ladder dangling from a ship seemed difficult enough. I tried to imagine what it would be like to leap from that small bobbing boat to the tiny platform of a ladder step hanging vertically from the rolling side of a moving ship. Even more difficult would be the leap from the ladder to the cushioned well which formed a catching area in the forward part of the daughter boat. Lifting boat, descending ladder; in that moment the jump would have to be made. It would take the agility of a young man to make the leap, the experience of years to land safely. I remembered what Tom had told me: one hundred practice trips before a man qualifies himself as a pilot. Where and how, I wondered, did he practice for the first one?

With the pilot safely delivered to the ship, one more maneuver is required before the operation is complete. The daughter boat must get back aboard its mother ship.

I have had some experience in handling small boats. Somehow it runs contrary to all that I know to deliberately plow into the stern of another boat. But that is how the daughter boat returns to its mother, along with a big wave under its bottom to help it climb up the ramp. It is the wave that carries the boat

safely over the stern transom of the *Columbia*. A quick-catch
hook holds the boat, the wave runs out, and all is secure. If
everything is timed just right, it works. If not, the boat either hits
the stern or is washed back to the sea by the retreating wave.

Andy described what it was like to come rushing up behind the *Columbia* on the crest of a twelve-foot wave, to look
down at the steel deck in front, and then to drive the boat full
speed down the front of the wave to hit the ship at the instant the
wave broke. He did not offer to let me try it.

The technology of the pilot service has vastly improved
since old Chief Comcomly put out in his canoe from Chinook
Point to pilot the ships of the Hudson's Bay Company across the
bar. Diesel engines have replaced sail. Satellites can forecast
weather. Electronic devices can pinpoint a vessel's position and
radios allow instant communication. But there is still that moment between pilot boat and ship where there is nothing but
ocean. It is a gap that must still be bridged by human hand, foot
and judgment.

Search, rescue, and save

Bᴀᴄᴋ ɪɴ ᴍʏ ʙᴏᴀᴛ, I crossed over the wide river mouth and tied up at the U.S. Coast Guard Station that lies in the protected lee of Cape Disappointment. The life-saving missions of the crews at this station are another part of Columbia River bar history and legends.

There was no organized life-saving system at the mouth

of the Columbia prior to 1865. In that year Joel Munson began a volunteer effort with a metal lifeboat he salvaged from the wreck of the sailing bark *Industry*. Munson organized a benefit dance in Astoria to raise money to equip this first boat, and free moorage was provided at Fort Canby in Baker Bay. Volunteer crews manned self-bailing rowboats until 1880.

On 4 May of that year, a severe storm caught the lower river fishing fleet in the exposed river and a number of fishermen drowned. As a result of this tragedy, an eight-man professional crew was hired by the U.S. government to man the Cape Disappointment lifeboat station.

After tying my boat to the station dock, I was escorted to the station administration office and introduced to Seaman Matt Goodrich, who was both a maintenance painter and public affairs officer for the base. He first showed me the rescue accident reports which are filed after each call for Coast Guard assistance. Each report profiles such information as the location of the distress call, time of day, number of lives lost or saved, property lost and recovered, and the time required for the search, the rescue and the follow up assistance.

What, I asked, is the major cause of accidents? Engine failures, Matt told me, account for ninety percent of the problems that happen. The engine failure in itself may not be important, he explained, but it frequently sets off a train of events which lead to more serious problems. Records show that very few recreational boaters cross the bar with any back-up options. Simple things, said Matt, that would save lives... things every boat should carry like a wrench, a spark plug, a fan belt and other small parts that could be used to make quick repairs.

The Coast Guard averages around 150 requests for assistance during the three winter months of December, January and February. River and bar traffic during this time is mostly commercial with vessels better equipped to handle emergencies and crews more experienced in rough water conditions. Requests for assistance increase dramatically with the opening of the summer sportfishing season. Five hundred calls during the three-month summer season is not at all unusual. Matt told me that in one recent thirty-day period, the station responded to three hundred distress calls. I figured it up; that month required a rescue or assistance mission every 2.4 hours.

Normally, two complete boat crews are kept on stand-by duty at the base. During peak periods of the recreational season, watches are doubled, boats are brought in from other bases and Coast Guard Auxiliary volunteers are called in for assistance. I was surprised that the waters of the lower river and the outside coast were the scene of so many boating accidents.

Matt pushed across the desk two large scrapbooks containing the pasted news clippings of Coast Guard rescue stories. They were dreary and monotonous reports of carelessness, faulty equipment, and poor judgment. I could read only a few out of hundreds.

Three men and a woman were plucked out of the water just off South Jetty after the 21 foot pleasure boat they were riding capsized. . . .

At Cape Disappointment, an 18 foot pleasure craft capsized near the tip of the north jetty and two people were reported to be in the water when a helicopter was dispatched. . . .

Two people were rescued Friday in a 16 foot boat that caught fire in the Pacific off Cape Disappointment. . . .

Between August 25 and August 31 the U.S. Coast Guard answered 56 calls for distress out of Cape Disappointment. Out of the calls, Coast Guardsmen aided 43 pleasure boats, one sailing vessel, nine fishing vessels and two charter boats with a total of 144 persons assisted. Saturday, Aug. 30 was the busiest day for the Coast Guard with 11 pleasure boats and one charter boat assisted with a total of 38 persons on board.

When conditions are too rough for recreational boats, the Coast Guard closes the bar and asks boaters to wait either inside or outside the bar until conditions improve. This would seem to be a reasonable and prudent request, but not all boaters see it that way. They interpret the closure as a curtailment of their liberties, sometimes as an insult to their seamanship abilities. The closure is often ignored.

Matt recalled one awful day of recent history. The bar had been closed at 10:00 A.M., leaving a number of small boats outside. The Coast Guard set up a patrol to keep them from entering the river until the ebb tide slackened and waves diminished. In spite of the closure, a number of the outside boats tried to evade the patrolling Coast Guard boats and run in. On just one wave, the patrolling boats picked up two dead bodies and rescued three other people from a swamping accident. The two people who drowned were in their eighties. Twice their boat had tried to enter the river and twice the Coast Guard escorted it back to sea. On the third attempt the boat went undetected by the patrol, was caught on a wave and swamped.

"What must I have aboard my boat to make it legal for me to cross the bar and go to sea?" I asked. The requirements are minimal: The boat must be licensed in my resident state and I must carry a Coast Guard-approved life jacket for each person aboard, a fire extinguisher, a horn or whistle, and a set of flares.

"With that, can I do as I damn please? Head to sea with grandma, wife and kids in a brand new boat in my first experience afloat?"

"The ocean is yours," said Matt.

"And you can't stop me from crossing the bar?"

"Only if we close the bar to everyone," he said.

"Do people think about where they are going? Do they know what the hazards might be? Do they wonder about what they are getting into?"

It was too many questions in a string. There was a long pause and Matt said without judgment or criticism, "They just want to get that fish; they just want to catch a salmon."

I was the one excited. "So what that the gas pump leaks a little, the bilge pump won't work, the engine runs a bit hot. Fix 'em later. For now, get the fish! Is that the background to all these accidents?"

Quietly Matt nodded his head. "Yep, that's it."

"If you rescue a person and his boat, what is the reaction?" I asked.

There was another thoughtful pause before Matt answered.

"Relief, gratitude. . . until." His voice trailed off and stopped.

"Until what?" Again, I pushed him to answers I knew he was uncomfortable with.

"Until we get inside where it's safe. Until we step aboard and begin asking questions. Until we begin to write up our report."

"Then what happens?"

"Well, once they are safe they begin to think back. 'That wasn't so bad. We did okay. Probably didn't need the Coast Guard after all.' Then we step aboard and ask questions. Often gratitude turns to a kind of hostility. We are only trying to get information. They think it some kind of governmental inquisition, that by being rescued they are guilty of something and open to criticism."

Matt's voice wandered off again. "It's strange. . . sometimes I just don't understand them."

My last question was a personal one.

"Winter time, big swells breaking. . . what's it really like out there?"

The answer was the simple statement from one who knows the bar, respects it and is not afraid to admit that he is sometimes afraid of it.

"It's really scary. Wind gusting maybe sixty, seventy miles an hour, swells breaking maybe fifteen, twenty feet high. Even on good boats like ours, which are nearly foolproof, it's really scary. It's also kind of thrilling. I don't like to rescue people in heavy weather but. . . well, I guess I like to be out there. Sometimes, anyhow.

"Usually, if someone drowns, they are dead before we are even notified. Since I have been here, we have never failed to bring back the boat and its passengers alive. . . if we have been notified. If someone has died, it's always been before the station was called. Since I've been here, anyway."

His answer was not a boast, but a qualified statement of the record. The next call could be different. Bragging doesn't count for much on the bar.

Fort Clatsop

IT WAS AN EASY WALK from the Coast Guard station to the summit of Cape Disappointment. Here I picked up the line of the second important journey to the Columbia River, the one that came overland under the command of Meriwether Lewis and William Clark.

The expedition reached the cape on 18 November 1805, to

37

conclude the first transcontinental crossing of North America. The journal described the expedition's condition at the conclusion of the long trek.

Nov. 28, 1805: Wind shifted about to the S.W. and blew hard accompanied with hard rain. rained all the last night we are all wet our bedding and Stores are also wet, we haveing nothing which is Sufficient to keep ourselves bedding or Stores dry,   O! how disagreeable is our Situation dureing this dreadfull weather.

Dec. 1, 1805: . . . Since we arrived in Sight of the Great Western; (for I cannot Say Pacific) Ocian as I have not Seen one pacific day Since my arrival in its vicinity, and its waters are forming and petially breake with emenc waves on the Sands and rockey coasts, tempestous and horiable.

The expedition had suffered severely from cold, rain and lack of food while traveling down the lower river. Two things were desperately needed; food and shelter. Standing on Cape Disappointment with the view of the entire lower river around me, I tried to work through the planning and logistics which confronted the expedition.

The party had followed the north shore of the river, a steep and inhospitable lee shore that lay continuously exposed to the forces of the cold, wet westerly and southwesterly winds blowing in from the ocean. A sheltered site was needed for the construction of a defensible winter headquarters where the party could rest and prepare for the long overland journey back across the continent.

The second requirement – food – was essential, not only on a daily basis, but as a reserve to be prepared for the homeward journey. The only dependable food sources were wild game, particularly deer and elk. The winter camp would have to be located close to a forest that contained these animals in abundance. The same forests that were the habitat for game, however, would be nearly impenetrable to a walking man. Game would be much easier to procure if it could be shot near a river and transported by canoe rather than backpacked over the land.

A winter headquarters, then, would have to be protected from the ocean winds, near a dependable supply of game and located on a small tributary river that would give access to the hunting grounds. The closest river noted by the expedition was the Cowlitz, upstream from Cape Disappointment. But, it was too far from the mouth of the Columbia, which the expedition wanted to keep under observation because of the possibility of a ship arrival. Where then, and quickly, to prepare a winter home? My eyes skirted the south shore of the river. There, in a low line of trees set back from what appeared to be a deep indentation of the shore, was a possible site. My chart identified it as Youngs Bay and flowing into its southwest corner was a river, the Lewis and Clark River.

I traveled slowly along the edge of the channel through the shallow water of Youngs Bay, trying to stay out of the midstream current. Gray-cloaked herons stalking the shallows served as my leadsmen as they sounded the water in front of me with their long stick legs. The exposed mudbanks of the shoreline were pocketed with thousands of small depressions and tiny rivulets which held the water of the last high tide. Swallows, diving for insects, dimpled the flat, silver-gray surface of the river. The sound of my engine was an intrusion in the early morning stillness. I regretted that I was not traveling by canoe to the site where Lewis and Clark built Fort Clatsop, the first American fort on the Pacific Northwest Coast.

From the river, it was apparent to me that the expedition had chosen a good site for Fort Clatsop. The Lewis and Clark River extends a few miles south from Youngs Bay through a flat marshland and then turns in a southeasterly direction along the base of a ridge of hills that stand between the river and the Pacific. The surface of the river was windless. The hillsides were heavily forested and elk, I knew, still wandered there. The site of

Fort Clatsop was selected not by accident, but by good judgment based on the necessities of survival.

Looking up from the river, I saw under the dark shadows of trees the hollowed-out shape of a log canoe lying in a clearing. I had reached the place called "Canoe Landing." The replica of the fort cannot be seen from the river. I tied my boat to a log raft and, carrying my shoes in my hand, stepped ashore through deep, soft mud. A carefully cut path led me up a hill beneath somber green trees. A few of those trees, I thought, were old enough to be living when Lewis and Clark passed this way.

My initial response to the fort was one of disappointment; it seemed so small, so low and so crude. The perimeter is formed by a continuous wall of logs standing upright in the ground. Inside this stockade, dirt-floored rooms huddle beneath a roof which rings the inside of the fort.

With constant rain and dripping trees, a colder, draftier, wetter, more dreary place was hard to imagine until I considered the expedition's alternative – no shelter at all. After more than a year of living in the open, the fort must have been a luxury to the wet and weary men. Here stood a room for storing wood, wood that could keep a man warm. And there, a row of bunks under a roof that protected him from the rain. The architecture of Fort Clatsop was one of economy and utility. It was designed as a mechanism for survival. It was built in less than a month and occupied for less than three. Abandoned, it returned to the loam of the forest before history resurrected it and made it a monument. It is to the West what Plymouth Rock is to the East. Both are shrines; the rock for a colony, the fort for the empire of the West.

Astoria

Lᴇᴡɪs ᴀɴᴅ Cʟᴀʀᴋ spent four Northwest winter months at the site of Fort Clatsop, and during that time they had only twelve days without rain. Just ten miles inland from the Pacific Ocean, Astoria knows that climate and endures it as the assault point for all the gathering storms brewed by the turbulent winds of the Northeast Pacific.

Weather sets the mood and the color of Astoria. You can watch the clouds approach, pass through, and then go scudding inland along the corridor of the river as a gray, dirty-white, and murky-black ceiling.

The *U.S. Coast Pilot*, the bible for marine weather data, reports sixty-six inches of annual rainfall in Astoria and skies overcast an average of 242 days out of the year. The greatest amount of monthly precipitation is a January record of nineteen inches. No month is without some rain, and the annual average humidity is seventy-nine with an average daily mean temperature of a cool 50.5 degrees. Visibility on forty-three days a year is a quarter of a mile or less.

I arrived on a summer day. It was wet, raining and cold. After tying up the boat, I headed uptown looking for the closest restaurant. The grand design of my voyage – to experience something of the conditions which had affected the history of the river – had driven me to a whimpering search for a cup of hot coffee. In the restaurant I talked with a young attorney who had just moved to Astoria to begin his new practice. I asked him if he was worried about starting a practice in a city that was again wandering in an economic lull.

"Not at all," he said. "Astoria has always been like this. Its advantage is that it has learned to live with a depression better than most places."

It was an attitude I found prevalent in the city; Astoria and hard times are old comrades.

Astoria is a peninsular city standing like a clenched fist between the waters of Youngs Bay and the main channel of the Columbia River. The shape of a fist could stand as a symbol for the city. Force it open and it would show the rough, callused, palm and fingers of a hand that have dug, chopped and pushed and pulled with shovel, axe, oar and saw to create some man's entrepreneurial vision of an empire. The work was there in the mills, the shipyards, the forests, along the channels of the river, and outward across the river bar. The flaw, perhaps, was that the vision represented moneyed interests far away from rough and tumble Astoria. The city began as an outpost of commerce, and as an outpost city it remains. Tough as a fist, stubborn, independent and, above all, proud. It has survived.

Astoria remembers its better days. Any oldtimer can tell you what it was like. The boats of the fishing fleet numbered in the thousands. The mills clanked and smoked round the clock, the whine of their headsaws never quiet. It was a time of simple faith: Nature would provide, man would harvest. It was the philosophy of the frontier, the promise of the American West. With hard work, luck and patience anything and everything was possible. Astoria, the oldest American settlement west of the Mississippi River, was the origin of that dream.

Astoria was to have been the center of an empire. It was the vision of the European-born John Jacob Astor (the first absentee owner of Astoria) who was able to conceive plans and actions on a global scale that crossed continents and linked nations. The reports of the Lewis and Clark expedition convinced Astor that a series of fur trading posts could be established along the upper Missouri and the Columbia rivers. Fort Astor was founded in 1811 to serve as the collection and shipping point for that fur enterprise. The market was China.

The concept of the plan projected lines of transport and supply that crossed North America, encircled South America and spanned the Pacific. It was a venture that touched and influenced the politics of the period. It was a plan dramatic and bold in concept and years ahead of its time in terms of communications, technology, administration and logistics. It failed, but because of it, the United States was able to strengthen its claim to the vast region known as the Oregon Territory. Astoria was the beginning of the American settlement of the West.

Fort Astor was sold to the British North West Company in 1813 and renamed Fort George. This company merged with the Hudson's Bay Company, and operations were moved to Fort Vancouver when Fort George was abandoned in 1825. In 1844, Astoria had four white citizens. One of them, John M. Shively, opened the first post office west of the Rockies in 1847.

The California gold rush and the San Francisco construction boom gave the settlement its first sustaining industry – logging and lumber. After the destruction of the salmon fishery on the Sacramento River by the gold mining operations, the Columbia River fishing industry began to grow, and Astoria became the center of this industry.

By the turn of the century, Astoria was a thriving city with a lusty, brawling, ethnic population of sailors, fishermen, cannery workers and loggers. Its shame and its pride was Astor Street, the city's red light district which boasted fifty-four saloons and thirty-five brothels. World War I created the city's shipbuilding industry and three yards operated in the area. The city reached its population peak in the early 1920s. After World War II, shipyards closed and Astoria's population began a slow but continuous decline. Today, its population is half of the post-World War I figure.

In 1922, nearly the entire downtown district of Astoria was destroyed by fire. A second fire that same year destroyed the city's largest sawmill and it was never rebuilt. World War II gave the city a short term economic boost, but the postwar period saw a steep decline in the resource-based industries of fish and lumber. As a port city, Astoria's shipping business fell far behind the upriver ports of Longview, Vancouver and Portland. An aluminum plant, an oil port, a coal-shipping center and other revitalizing industries have been proposed for Astoria, but none have ever materialized.

Resignation is the obvious reaction to such a litany of economic hopes lifted and then shattered. To a considerable extent, Astoria has never really been able to enjoy the freedom of shaping its own future. This has been done by the price set on fish and lumber outside the area, and by decisions made in corporate boardrooms in New York, San Francisco and Portland. The absentee ownership of Fort Astor by John Jacob Astor in New York has continued down to this day, and Astoria is still operated as a corporate outpost. Decisions made elsewhere set Astorians to working overtime, half-time or no time at all.

Leaving the restaurant, I visited the office of Paul Benoit, director of the research and planning organization called CREST (Columbia River Estuary Study Task). I asked Paul if Astoria's old history stood in the way of its future.

"Yes," he replied. "It's produced an attitude accepted by many people that Astoria is just a place that is traditionally down and out."

Benoit sees Astoria as a place bound by its own traditions. He cited the salmon industry as an example.

"The whole industry is now artificial," he believes, "and it would not stand up to a cost-benefit analysis. What we are trying to save is not an economic system but a way of life."

What he sees as necessary is a renewal of the industry through different attitudes towards fish and fishing; opportunities that might present themselves if the industry could break away from the diminished salmon resource and the tradition of harvesting fish with a boat and a hook or net.

When Benoit first arrived in Astoria, he saw all the diked fields of the river's largely abandoned lowland dairy farms and at first assumed that they were fish farms similar to ones he had seen in the Orient. He thinks that it might be possible that these diked fields could be converted to aquaculture.

"I'm not saying that they could. I'm suggesting that it is an idea that could be tried. Instead of building dikes and tide gates to keep water out, it would seem that the process could be reversed and at very little cost the fields could be flooded for fish farming."

Salmon raised in a cow pasture? The idea seemed to me absurd until Benoit pointed out that he was not talking about the high-cost species of salmon and steelhead, but about the kind of fish that most of the world's populations eat – carp, eel, catfish, crayfish – the kind of fish that could find a ready market in China and Japan and with the growing Asian populations of the United States.

"But salmon. . . ," Benoit paused as he swung his chair

towards the window to look out at the dreary rain-washed sky-line of downtown Astoria.

"Salmon may just not be the way of the future. If that resource, and the lumber resource, were still strong, Astoria's history would give the area a progressive lead over every other area because of its experience and ability to develop new tech-nologies and techniques. But as it is, with the base of life sort of dripping away, people here are left twiddling their thumbs."

Benoit sees in Astoria's historic view of itself a future tourist opportunity, a future that would not have to lose its sense of the past. He calls it a "vital mix," something that Astoria could become without losing its history. People don't want, he be-lieves, Astoria's old waterfront to become just another tourist development where something artificial is created for the tourist with no reference to history or tradition.

"People here," he said, "see Astoria for what it has always been, a working waterfront, and that is the way they want to keep it."

Later in the day, as I sloshed along that waterfront in rub-ber boots past a fish cannery, two marine stores, warehouses, a tugboat dock, and the imposing building of the Columbia River Maritime Museum, I shuddered at the thought of these places being dolled up for the tourist with stores selling souvenirs of things that had never existed and imported gimcracks that no one needed.

Astoria, I thought, *could* be different, something other than the banal and the trivial, a clutter of the chic, the useless, and the artificial. Something other than an arcade of stores and shops that would obliterate behind false fronts the dignity, history and tradition of honest work in a very old river town that looks out-ward to the sea.

Such a place is the Astoria Marine Construction Com-pany, a collection of huge open sheds standing on the east bank of the Lewis and Clark River, just west of the city. From these buildings and ways came the ships, barges, fishboats, and tugs employed by marine enterprises all along the Pacific Coast.

I tied my boat to a half–sunk dock and walked through the yards. An old man was driving wooden plugs into the rub strake of a fishboat. A long-haired youth was patiently sanding the hull of another boat. The huge sheds stood open and empty. In dark corners, the massive shapes of bandsaws, planners, and forges stood dust-covered and silent. I wandered through the yard past empty cable reels, old engine parts, crab traps, and piles of timbers to reach the yard office where I introduced myself to the owner-manager, Don Fastabend.

Proudly, Don Fastabend told me he built his business with his "hands and two bits." He had acquired the yard several years ago, and before he became owner he had worked in the yard as a boat builder. With equal pride he showed me a collection of old photographs of the ships and boats built in the yard during its busy days. It was as though he was showing me an album of his family pictures. Each boat was recalled with a story and remembered by name to give a record of continuity to his life, a recorded history of accomplishment in the building of the boats.

Like most things in Astoria, the yard had seen better times, and it now exists largely on boat repair work. But Don Fastabend, native Astorian, keeps an occupation in reserve. He owns a fishboat and drift rights to his piece of the river. Fishing is how he grew up, and to fishing he can return. With hands, two bits and a fishboat, Fastabend believes a man can survive.

It was dusk as I headed back towards Astoria in my boat. Behind me, a gentle curving bridge arched over the Lewis and Clark River, its green, lifting span rusting as it waited to open for ships that no longer pass. All around me on the river shore the past lay crumbling in the ruins of old docks, pilings, weathered barns, and falling fences.

Ahead of me, Astoria was a glittering hillside of lights surrounded by a crimson river reflecting a setting sun on the horizon of the sea. City, river, ocean, and a backdrop of black-green hills; what more, I thought, could a place be? Benoit was right. Astoria's future is what it has always been – a place that stirs men's dreams with visions of things possible.

It waits only to again be discovered.

Forgotten shores

Aᴳᴀɪɴ, ɪ ᴄʀᴏꜱꜱᴇᴅ ᴛʜᴇ ʀɪᴠᴇʀ to reach its north shore. A summer storm made that crossing in my small boat something of a challenge. I laid a course that followed the shortest distance between Hammond on the Oregon shore and Chinook Point on the Washington side.

Nervously I set out wondering: Will the weather get

worse? Did I read the tide table correctly? Will I beat the incoming ship across the channel? Will the engine keep going?

For a long while the receding shoreline was still the closest land, the shore I could return to in the event of trouble. The
halfway point was when both shores were equally blurred. At
the midpoint, I no longer looked back. Slowly I closed with
shallow Baker Bay on the north shore, where I promptly ran
aground. How ridiculous I must have appeared as I waded
through the mud-filled bay towing the boat behind me. Sometimes the boat floated. Sometimes it just slithered forward in the
mud. The chart read three feet, two feet, one foot and then zero.
At zero, the boat and I were stuck, so I retraced my steps until the
water came to the level of my knees. I knew that the drivers of
the cars that looked down on me from the highway were saying,
"Look at the silly fool. Lost the channel and got stuck in the mud.
Serves him right." How could I explain to them that I was on a
river voyage of exploration, and that I had become stuck in the
mud because I was following an old chart that showed Baker
Bay as an anchorage area for ships.

One of the ships, the *Jenny*, a Bristol trader commanded
by James Baker, was the second ship to enter the Columbia. The
third ship, the *Chatham*, under command of William Broughton,
was ordered by Vancouver to explore the river Vancouver had
missed on his survey voyage north in 1792. Broughton entered
the river in October of that year and found Baker already at
anchor in the bay which Broughton named for him.

Baker Bay might have sheltered Fort Astor if the irascible
Jonathan Thorn, captain of the Fort Astor supply ship *Tonquin*,
had had his way.

Thorn had been contracted to haul supplies and person-
nel around Cape Horn for the establishment of the fort. The
Astor colony people traveled as passengers, and Thorn, a harsh,
authoritative disciplinarian, objected to their interference with
his command. Thorn lost the eight men he sent ahead in small
boats to sound the channel across the bar. Once inside the river,
he wanted to unload what he called his "lubberly" passengers as

quickly as he could so that he could begin a more profitable trading voyage north along the coast. Duncan McDougall, commander of the expedition, insisted that the south shore of the river offered a more favorable site for the post, and so the center of activity began and continued to develop on the Oregon side of the river.

Not much happened along the north shore for the next thirty years, until the Hudson's Bay Company built a trading store at the old Indian village on Chinook Point. In 1840, Captain James Scarborough, a retired Hudson's Bay Company pilot, carved out a land claim from Indian lands, married an Indian woman, and built one of the early showplace homes of the lower river at Baker Bay. The 820-foot-high hill rising behind Chinook Point bears his name.

This hill and the surrounding land had been the ancestral home of the Comcomly family, a distinguished branch of the Chinook tribe. The famous one-eyed chief was a trusted friend of the Astor colony and, as mentioned earlier, the first river pilot. When the old chief died, his head was impolitely separated from his body and sent to England for study and examination. The head eventually found its way back to Astoria where it reposed for a century in the city's archives. It was finally returned to tribal descendants of the family, who met and accepted it at the last meeting of the Chinook tribe on 18 January 1953 in Skamokawa, Washington.

Today – as I discovered while wading through the mud – the old rendezvous of explorer and trader ships is a shoal water bay barely deep enough to float the sixteen-foot boat of a curious river traveler.

Once more I drifted in my boat just inside the mouth of the Columbia and below the cliff of Cape Disappointment, while I sipped a morning cup of coffee and waited for the return of the flood tide. The voyage I had begun a week earlier had returned me to the point of its beginning. Slowly the tide turned, and currents carried the boat upriver toward a journey along the Columbia's forgotten lower shore, a place where years ago time stopped and then turned backward.

Two cultures, Indian and white, have lived along these shores. Both survived by fishing, and both lived in small communities located along the river edge. Copies of two old maps I carried with me showed the locations of numerous lower river white communities which, nearly site for site, were built over the ruins of the older Indian settlements. Examples are:

WHITE COMMUNITY	INDIAN COMMUNITY
Ilwaco	Uitshutk
Wallicut	Qwatsamuts
Stringtown	Waphlutsin
Chinook	Clakhahl
McGowan	Kekaiugilhum
Chinookville	Qaiiltsiuk
Oneida	Moqwul
Eden	Nakathiqi
Carlson's Landing	Tlalegak
Pillar Rock	Chakwayalham
Skamokawa	Tlashgenemaki

Of the Indian communities, nothing remains. All that is left of most of the white communities are the broken stubs of old river pilings; evidence that these settlements once existed. A few places linger on – Altoona, Chinook, Skamokawa and, of course, the larger towns of Ilwaco and Cathlamet – but most have faded into obscurity, casualties of the fishing resource that dwindled, the highways that passed them by, and the old folks who died without need to be replaced.

Ilwaco

ILWACO IS ONE OF THE PLACES that has hung on, and I remember visiting there years ago. It was a commercial fishing town, and not much else. The old docks of its harbor sheltered one of the largest fishing fleets along the coast. You could walk those docks at your pleasure, inspect the boats, wonder about the complexity of their gear and equipment, and listen to fishermen grumble, curse, tell jokes on each other, and laugh.

A harborside boatyard was always busy building and re-pairing boats. It gave off the most wonderful smells; the pungent odor of red lead paint and tar mixed with a dash of rotting sea-weed and the fragrance of woodchips. Uptown Ilwaco consisted of several good, serious drinking bars, a couple of restaurants that served huge breakfasts to booted fishermen, and a hard-ware and general goods store that stocked everything worth having – fishing gear, guns, tools, hardware, and woolen out-door clothing.

Ilwaco was a landsman's contact with the sea and its peo-ple; their crafts and their boats. As a visitor, you were tolerated and politely ignored by a group of rough, hard-drinking, hard-working, proud men who went their way with a spirit of gusto and independence. The air was fresh, the wind blew hard and the cries of the sea gulls were deafening. Ilwaco was a fisherman's fishing port and the rest of the world could go to hell. I loved the smelly old place.

But then it changed and became a different Ilwaco. Its streets became jammed with cars, pickup trucks, recreation vehicles, people, children, and dogs. The waterfront was a clustered row of charter boat offices decorated with a litter of signs and strings of fluttering plastic flags. The screech of the gulls was drowned by stereo music and the shouting of a public address system announcing the latest winners in a continuous fishing contest.

Ilwaco was still a fishing town, but its new fishermen were the tourists who came to catch sport fish aboard the bright new charter boats with catchy names that lined the harbor. For forty dollars anyone – man, woman, or child – could be a fisherman, climb aboard a boat and go to sea. They came from upriver towns and from inland cities, and paid to have their hooks baited, their fish landed, cleaned and photographed, canned and packaged.

It was a profitable new fishing industry. New restaurants opened. Saloons were painted and became cocktail lounges. Motel and trailer parks were built. The old dock was replaced by a modern marina. Ilwaco's old fishermen made way for the new tourist fishermen in the new town.

A few summers ago, on a different trip, I again visited the town, arriving by boat. The harbor was strangely quiet and deserted. A posted notice advised me that I would be fined ten dollars unless I registered at the port office. The port office was closed and so was the restaurant next to it. Behind garbage cans, rusting boat trailers, and a truck with a flat tire, I searched for some kind of registration book or box. Nothing was to be found, no one was about.

Uptown, the streets were nearly empty. Plastic pennants hung limply in the moist evening air. Two customers were silhouetted in the dim window of a harborside restaurant. Across the street was the town's one bright place, the white glare of an empty pizza parlor. At a newspaper box, I bought a copy of the 3 August 1982 issue of the Oregon *Journal*. Under a streetlight I read the headline:

"Fish Closure Puts Ilwaco Up for Sale."

Below the headline, the story reported that the recent curtailment of sportfishing had crippled the town, forcing the closure of many restaurants, bank repossession of many charter boats, and the posting of a sign that read "Town for Sale."

I had arrived at a port of disaster. A recent crackdown by game wardens on fish limits had resulted in a suspension of sportfishing, and the new industry had come to a standstill. The closure had interrupted what Ilwaco called the "World's Greatest Salmon Derby." I read about the derby in an issue of the Chinook *Observer* that morning at breakfast. Said the article about the conclusion of the derby:

the young fishermen received their awards as champions including a fishing patch and a knowledge of what is happening to our fishing rights. This is what the derby is all about, to make it possible for you and young Americans to fish in the future.

I wondered as I read the article how a derby put fish in the river for future young Americans to catch. The story did not explain this perplexity, but went on to report that an "army of wardens" had appeared in Ilwaco and "abused the people to the point where they showed real fear, a real fear not usually seen in America. It was similar to the tactics of Germany's Gestapo in World War II."

Our fish. Our rights. Our American rights. These are old claims along the lower shores of the Columbia River. By such rights the Indians were killed off, the trees stripped from the hills, and the fish taken from the river. The nearly deserted lower river shore is evidence of how such rights are concluded; no industry, no future, no people. Ilwaco was not to be blamed; it was merely the most recent victim in the conflict of claims to the river's resources.

Leaving the town behind me, I cleared the harbor and headed across the mudflats of Baker Bay. I picked my way through a slalom field of abandoned pilings that dated from the time when the bay and its island, Sand Island, were ringed by the fence-like salmon traps of an earlier fishing technology.

Sand Island, though nearly joined to the Washington shore at low tide, is actually part of Oregon. The old dividing line between the two states followed the early ship channel which ran north of Sand Island. Over the years, the island slowly moved north, still carrying the flag of Oregon ownership as it migrated across the river.

In 1896, the island was occupied by federal troops sent to quell a bitter feud between gillnet fishermen and local cannery owners. The canneries had built the fish traps along the shores of the bay and the island on sites claimed by the gillnetters. A few shots were fired, and the event made newspaper headlines as a "fish war." The issue was finally settled in favor of the fish trap owners and this efficient method of taking salmon continued until outlawed by the state of Washington in 1934. (The state of Oregon banned the use of fish traps in 1926.)

Chinookville, now an abandoned site, was the center of the fish trap industry. For centuries, the land around the community had been the ancestral home and fishing grounds of the Chinook Indians. An early land promoter, Washington Hall, claimed the land in 1848, despite the resistance of the still-remaining members of old Chief Comcomly's clan. Hall was able to maintain his claim by fencing off the tribe's accustomed source of fresh water. Oregon settlers had arrived before federal laws offered some protection of Indian rights, so no one contested the removal of a few Indians whose only claim to the land was tradition.

Hall platted his town, and it grew to become the county seat of Pacific County. The location of old Chinookville does not appear on today's maps and charts, but it was located near McGowan, which can be seen on present-day charts. McGowan can be identified from the river or the highway by the spire of the St. Mary's church. The church dates back to the late 1840s when Fathers Toussaint Mesplie and Joseph Linnet moved into the area and opened the Stella Maris mission. Few Indians were converted by the Catholic priests, and the land was later purchased in 1853 by a man who played a significant role in the history of the lower river – Patrick McGowan.

McGowan was one of the first salmon processors on the lower river. He began by salting the salmon to preserve them, and then quickly changed to the canning method when this process was developed in 1884. The company eventually moved to Ilwaco where it continued operations until the early 1950s.

In 1864, U.S. Army Captain George Elliot negotiated a purchase of the Scarborough family land claim that covered much of Chinook Point and Scarborough Hill. The land was purchased for the construction of Fort Columbia, the third fort in the Columbia River defense plan laid out by the war department for the protection of the river entry. Two of the installations were already in place, one at Point Adams on the southern shore of the river, and the other at Cape Disappointment. The assumed enemy was at first the warships of foreign nations and, later, Confederate gun boats.

The land for Fort Columbia stood vacant until the outbreak of the Spanish-American War, and it was not until 1903 that the fort was garrisoned. None of the three forts ever fired at an enemy vessel.

Chinook

BY GUESSWORK AND GOOD LUCK, I missed holing the boat on one of Baker Bay's hundreds of underwater pilings and eventually I found my way to the dredged channel of deeper water which led me to the little rock-walled harbor of Chinook. I found the port captain in a small shack at the edge of the parking lot, which carried on its unpainted wall a sign reading "office." He took my four dollars, put the money in a cigar box, and told me to "park anywhere." He then returned to the conversation I had interrupted with an old crony seated in a splay-legged wicker chair.

I appreciated his matter-of-fact, noncurious welcome. It made me feel at ease. I didn't have to explain myself or my boat, where I had come from, or where I was going. To the port captain, I was just one more person traveling the river. If I paid my four dollars I could spend the night. If not, I could push off at my leisure.

Walking uptown, I inquired about the location of the local liquor store at a gas station.

"Don't have one," I was told by the attendant. "Chinook's not really a town. We never incorporated. Never thought we had to."

At the post office, I asked the trim lady behind the counter if she was the postmistress.

"No," she answered, "I'm the postmaster."

I apologized for my mistake and asked her if she could direct me to someone who might be able to tell me a little about the history of Chinook.

"That would be Mel Lebeck," she told me. Mel Lebeck, she explained, was born in Chinook, grew up with the fishing industry, and had only recently retired as manager of the Chinook Packing Plant. "House is just up the road. New house on the right side of the highway. Can't miss it."

I walked along the highway on a footpath past green strips of grass fronting neatly painted houses, trim gardens, and flower-hidden fences. Every driveway, garage, shed, vacant lot, and brush patch had its boat on a trailer or turned upside down against the weather. Stacks of wood were piled against the houses, salvage from the backyard beaches visible between each house.

Everyone knew where Mel Lebeck lived. On my way to his house, I gathered odd bits of information as I asked for further directions. I learned the name of a flower I admired, got the weather report for the next two days, was given the cost of a roof being repaired, and the age of an old gillnet boat falling to pieces under a tree. It was all idle gossip with strangers, but at the end of my walk to Mel Lebeck's house, I was beginning to feel very much at home in Chinook.

I found Mel Lebeck (the two names were always pronounced together) reading on the wide deck in back of his house. The house overlooks the entire lower river; the bar, Cape Disappointment, Point Adams, and the distant line of the Oregon shore. In his retirement years, Mel Lebeck has settled down with a view of the geography of his life's work. Looking off into that view, he told me that he began as a boat puller and retired as manager of the cannery that at one time bought the fish he caught.

He told me the cannery was started in 1915 by Albion Gile. Gile had come by ship to Willapa Bay to cut timbers for a dock he was building in San Francisco. For some reason, the ship's cook felt that he been cheated out of some of the profits of the venture, and he set fire to the ship. Gile was left stranded on the shores of the bay, without his ship, and broke. Looking around for a new venture, he began harvesting the abundant oysters in Willapa Bay, which he arranged to ship to San Francisco. The operation prospered, and he then moved into the salmon canning business by opening the Chinook Packing Plant. This cannery, said Mel Lebeck, is still operating and is the oldest cannery on the river.

I told him that I felt an atmosphere in Chinook completely different from the one I felt in Ilwaco, just a few miles down the road. I mentioned that the two places had nearly identical backgrounds and resources and had been settled by the same strains of ethnic and religious cultures at about the same time. Ilwaco had become a fair-sized town. Chinook had never grown beyond an unincorporated community.

"I guess we like it that way," was his explanation. He went on to point out that most of the homes in Chinook are fairly old, and that they were all built at about the same time. Not much has changed since then. He believed that some communities reach a kind of a peak and then go downhill. Chinook reached a kind of plateau and has remained there, not growing, not shrinking, but still very much alive with the second and third generations of the founding families.

"You know," said Lebeck, "we have never been very successful in organizing a Boy Scout troop here."

"Why not?" I asked, thinking that I just might have uncovered some flaw in Chinook's sense of community service.

"Because everything the Scouts could do for a boy, he can do for himself right in his own backyard."

Below the deck, a long beach was exposed by the low tide. Drift logs lay embedded in the sand. A few boats were pulled up on the beach, the curve of their transoms turned to the setting afternoon sun. Beyond, black, broken pilings poked above sun-golden mudflats and veined channels of bright water. The horizon was open to the sea, and I could imagine the pleasures and adventures of boyhood in a place like Chinook, a Tom Sawyer-town on the shore of the Columbia.

Chinook has a youth program all of its own. It is called "Sea Resources," and it is the nonprofit effort of Lebeck and other local people to operate a salmon hatchery. Its objectives are to increase salmon stocks and, more importantly, education. In the previous year, Lebeck said the hatchery released three million fish for a future commercial fish harvest. On-site classes for nearby high school students demonstrate and teach the traditional crafts of net mending, crab pot construction, and fishboat handling. All subjects illustrate the idea that fish are a resource that cannot be harvested without conservation and renewal. The operation takes as its theme Lebeck's simple philosophy about fish and the industries it supports: "Use nature itself to lay the plan."

Our talk drifted to the difficulties of the charter boat business in Ilwaco and the recent problems the city was having in paying off the huge loan it had borrowed to build the new marina to accommodate the fleet.

"The charter boats never moved in here," he said. "They were not wanted. Chinook is a commercial fishing town."

It was a simple description of Chinook, a statement that summarized what the community had always been – a place that looked to itself and to the river for its needs and its future. Chinook will never be put up "for sale."

Point Ellice

THE NEXT MORNING I LEFT CHINOOK, retraced the channel back into the main river, and headed upstream along the Washington shore towards Point Ellice. Point Ellice is the northern landing point for the 3.5 mile Astoria bridge. The bridge climbs up from the Astoria waterfront in a high arch that spans the main shipping channel, drops down to a long flat run across the shallows of Desdemona Sands, and then bulges upward again over North Channel before ending at the point.

Passing under the bridge, I recalled a time when I was caught in a small boat in the fast ebb tide flowing beneath the bridge, helpless because my outboard engine had stalled, and terrified that the current would carry the boat to disaster on the upstream side of one of the north shore jetties. Cars on the bridge above me traveled back and forth oblivious to my plight, windows rolled up, heaters on, and radios droning soft music as I drifted under the bridge helpless and out of control. There was nothing anybody could do for me, of course, but I remember cursing the aloofness of the bridge, an impersonal thing a person could cross in a car without regard for tide or current, wind or storm; the river below a thing to be forgotten behind the next curve.

It was at Point Ellice that the Lewis and Clark party spent some of their most anxious hours of the entire expedition. A terrible storm blocked further downriver passage and, reports the journal for 10 November 1805, the party was forced to camp on floating logs because the steepness of the shore afforded no campsite.

. . . the hills being either a perpendicular clift, or Steep assent, riseing to about 500 feet. our canoes we Secured as well as we could. we are all wet the rain haveing continued all day, our beding and maney other articles, employ our Selves drying our blankets. nothing to eate but dried fish pounded which we brought from the falls. we made 10 miles to day.

11 November: The expedition remained at Point Ellice with this entry in the journal.

A hard rain all the last night, dureing the last tide the logs on which we lay was all on float . . . rain falling in torrents, we are all wet as usial – and our Situation is truly a disagreeable one; the great quantites of rain which has loosened the Stones on the hill Sides; and the Small stones fall down upon us, our canoes at one place at the mercy of the waves, our baggage in another; and our selves and party Scattered on floating logs and Such dry Spots as can be found on the hill sides, and crivicies of the rocks.

12 November:

. . . our Situation is dangerous . . . all wet and colde . . . bedding is rotten . . . [a canoe] Split in her bottom.

It was not until 15 November that Clark was able to report the party's escape from Point Ellice.

. . . about 3 oClock the wind luled, and the river became calm, I had the canoes loaded in great haste and Set Out, from this dismal nitich where we have been confined for 6 days passed, without the possibility of proceeding on, returning to a better Situation, or get out to hunt . . .

The "nitich" described by Clark, a small indentation of the river shore just upstream from Point Ellice, became the ferry landing of Megler. The fenced and paved parking lot of a state park now covers the old terminal location, but no marker or plaque describes for the tourist the colorful era of the lower river ferry boats.

Solomon Smith, the first settler of the Clatsop Plains, began a ferry service in 1840 when he tied two canoes together and transported passengers and freight across the river. The first regular ferry service across the river was started after World War I by Captain Fritz Elfving, who built *Tourist I* to carry both passengers and automobiles. *Tourist I* could carry fourteen cars. By 1931, Elfving had three ferries in operation. The service was sold to the Oregon State Highway Commission in 1946. Two years later, the forty-four-car-capacity *M.R. Chessman*, named for the long-time editor of the *Astorian Budget*, was put into service. The *Kitsap* was launched in 1963, just three years before the $24 million bridge made the ferry service obsolete. During the highway commission's period of ferry service, the boats carried 5.5 million passengers and 2.5 million cars.

My first river trips were made on the old ferries. The ferry crossing was the highlight of our annual summer trip to Seaview, the old beach community north of Ilwaco. To a boy of eight or nine, that four mile crossing was a sea voyage. Frequently, the passage was rough enough to confine my parents to the shelter of their parked car. Freed from their supervision, I walked back and forth on the top deck of the ferry, bow to stern, stern to bow, to take in the wonderful views of the bow wash and destination ahead, and the stern wake and retreating shoreline behind.

Hungry Harbor

THE HIGHWAY CONSTRUCTED alongside the river upstream from Point Ellice and Megler has straightened out the steep river shore and filled in the few small natural coves that once offered some shelter to a boat caught out in rough weather. At the small inlet my chart identified as "Hungry Harbor," I stopped for lunch.

It got its name in the last century when a number of the old sailing gillnet boats took shelter from a storm in the cove. The storm lasted almost a week. The fishermen ran out of food and were unable to land their boats. From this ordeal the place was named.

Anchored in Hungry Harbor on a warm sunny morning as I ate cheese, fresh bread, and nibbled at a bunch of grapes, I remembered what an old gillnet fishermen had told me: "The best thing about the old days is that they are gone."

Knappton

JUST UPRIVER FROM HUNGRY HARBOR lies a silted, half-circle bay about two miles wide. Old pilings standing in neat, orderly lines across the shallow water of the bay are like tombstones to the memory of Knappton, once one of the lower river's oldest and largest sawmill and lumber docks. For some seventy years the whine of the saws was a continuous, round-the-clock noise in Knappton as timber was cut and shipped to markets on four continents.

Old photographs show tall, square-rigged ships and four-masted schooners tied to long docks, waiting to take on cargos of timbers, planks, and boards cut from the trees of the Washington hills. A busy community lived and worked within the shadow of the mill smoke. The photographs also show rows of company bunk houses, a hotel, a school, a store, and a post office that fronted the wooden sidewalks of the town.

The sawmill was the second venture developed by Jabez Burrell Knapp in the community bearing his name. His first operation, a cement plant, failed. In 1870 he founded the Columbia Saw Mill. It operated until 12 July 1941, when a disastrous fire destroyed both the mill and the town. Neither were ever rebuilt.

Carlton E. Appelo is a lower river historian and a native of the area. His profiles recording the history of some of the lower river communities have appeared in the telephone books of Wahkiakum County. History is indebted to him for the information he has assembled about the people and events of these early communities.

In *The Knappton Story*, he describes the insular climate of these villages. Though located on the mainland of the river shore, they looked to the river for all transportation, commerce, and communication with other villages. The life of each town revolved around the arrival and departure of the ferries. Wrote Appelo: "Each community was an island unto itself. Each made its own recreation and social life. Most were relatively self sufficient."

Appelo, who was born in a fishboat that was carrying his expectant mother to a hospital in Astoria, said that the introduction of the internal combustion engine changed the way of life for the lower river communities.

Soon there was incessant demand for year-round highways to replace the casual summer roads that were scarcely more than cow trails in this locality. The insular life began to evolve into something larger. The orientation was changing from a marine outlook on the mighty Columbia as the only avenue of communication and transportation – a carryover from the earliest Indian days – to a new vision of highways and byways, shifting the focus to the land mass. Up to this time, communities grew in relations to their proximity to the river frontage. Land transportation freed economies from the river.

From the old Knappton site, the highway turns to run inland behind the steep hills that border the Washington shore. It does not reappear again until it reaches the old town of Skamokawa, twenty-six miles upriver. Along that shoreline, today nearly deserted and roadless, my chart showed the sites of eleven old villages that at one time were the thriving communities of Appelo's history books. I matched the old chart with a modern river chart and headed upriver to explore the forgotten north shore.

Grays Bay

GRAYS BAY IS A PLACE that catches and holds the very special light of the lower river, a kind of muzzy glow of gray rain clouds backlighted by an occasional breakthrough of the sun. I crossed the bay looking out through a windshield spattered by rain drops that ran in shiny wind-streaked rivulets down the glass. A shaft of sunlight pierced the clouds and the river turned a lustrous silver. The sunlight faded and then the river darkened to the color of pewter. The encircling shore of the bay became a low, black smudge that ringed my boat in a misty island of water.

I went to the very middle of the bay and anchored in a full-circle exposure to whatever weather would come with the night. Inside my small cabin I had a lantern, a book, a bottle of sherry, a steaming stew, and a snug bed. With all those comforts, I felt sorry for the poor people who had to spend the wet night ashore.

If the lower Columbia had its ghosts, they would hover wraith-like in the mists of Grays Bay, their presence a convocation of the large events that shaped the river's history. By squinting my eyes a bit to close off the clear-cut area on the hills and the navigation marker on Rocky Point, I was able to visualize the landscape viewed by Gray when he anchored here in 1792. I would not have been surprised to have seen an Indian crossing the bay in a log canoe, heading for a shore that revealed only the smoke of its hidden plank-house village.

The name "Shallow Nitch" was given to the bay by Lewis and Clark. On Grays Point at the western edge of the bay, the expedition first encountered the terrible winter weather of the Northwest Coast. Journal entries for the dates of 8 and 9 November 1805, describe the condition of the party as it lay storm-bound on the point.

Swells or Waves so high that we thought it imprudent to proceed . . . we are all wet and disagreeable, as we have been for Several days past, and our present Situation a verry disagreeable one is as much as we have not leavel land Sufficient for an encampment and for our baggage to lie cleare of the tide, the High hills jutting in so close and steep that we cannot retreat back, and the water of the river too Salt to be used, added to this the waves are increasing to Such a hight that we cannot move from this place, in this Situation we are compelled to form our camp between the hite of the Ebb and flood tides, and rase our baggage on logs.

9 November: The expedition remained stormbound on Grays Point.

The tide of last night obliged us to unload all the canoes one of which sunk before she was unloaded by the high waves of swells which accompanied the returning tide, The others we unloaded, and 3 others was filled with water soon after by the swells or high sees which broke against the shore imediately where we lay, rained hard all the fore part of the day, the [tide] which rose untill 2 oClock p m to day brought with it such emence swells or waves, aded to a hard wind from the south which loosened the drift trees which is verry thick on the shore, and tossed them about in such a manner, as to endanger our canoes very much, with every exertion and the strictest attention by the party was scercely sufficient to defend our canoes from being crushed to pieces between those emencly large trees maney of them 200 feet long and 4 feet through . . . not withstanding the disagreeable time of the party for several days past they are all chearfull and full of anxiety to see further into the Ocian, the water is too salt to drink, we use rain water. The salt water has acted on some of the party already as a Pergitive. rain continues.

Frankfort

AFTER A STORMY NIGHT ON GRAYS BAY, I awoke the next morning and ate my breakfast while looking out at Portugese Point. It shelters a thin line of beach pushed close to the river edge by an advancing line of trees and brush. Except for a cautious deer, I had the view all to myself. The town that once occupied the beach has returned to the loam of the forest, and nothing remains of the great seaport planned for Grays Bay except the record that the place once existed; a courthouse deed dated November 1876 and signed by President Ulysses S. Grant, and the name, Frankfort, which appears on a few old maps of the lower river.

The deed was issued to one Barney Gallagher. It was later purchased by two Franks – Frank Bourn and Frank Scott. From their two names, they formed the Frankfort Land and Improvement and Investment Company in 1890. In that year the town of Frankfort was platted, and a sales office was opened in Portland to promote the new town. It was advertised in a 23 December 1890 edition of the *Oregonian* as a city that would have "harbor facilities unexcelled anywhere on the Pacific Coast north of San

Francisco." The ad boasted that the new city would soon "assume an important position among the cities of the most prosperous state in the union."

Frankfort did enjoy a few boom years. It acquired a post office, newspaper, school, hotel, saloon, and its own sternwheeler, proudly called *The City of Frankfort*, which offered service to and from Astoria. A depression in 1893 ended Frankfort's first three years of prosperity.

Hopes for the town were revived with a 1906 announcement in the Willapa *Harbor Pilot* of a new dream that read "Hill Plans Metropolis Near Mouth of River. Grays Bay is Chosen. All Surrounding Land Purchased by the G.N. and N.P." (Great Northern and Northern Pacific railroads). The news story stated that railroad magnate James Hill had purchased all the land surrounding Grays Bay to build a town to be called St. James. It was to be "the ultimate metropolis of the coast." Docks and a dredged harbor were planned and architects were instructed to design a hotel that would rival anything on the coast. But nothing came of all the plans for Frankfort. It survived as a fishing village until World War II, but it never had a road or electricity. The old Norwegian fisherman, Ole Levick, was its last resident. He died there in 1964, and the forest reclaimed Frankfort.

Deep River

AFTER BREAKFAST, I pulled up my anchor, and with the tide and wind pushing me, I drifted soundlessly into Brix Bay at the mouth of Deep River. Long ribbons of open water wandered aimlessly through silvered channels between bent stalks of waving green grass. Ducks lined up in front of me like tethered decoys facing the wind.

A line of red buoys marked the right edge of the channel that led me to Deep River. The river made a sharp left turn and ran beneath green tree branches that skimmed the surface of the water. Coming around a curve in the river, the line of deserted houses I saw squatting on the ruined piles of an old dock showed me that Deep River was another closed chapter in the history of the Columbia River.

Finnish emigrants first arrived in the area around 1875. Names such as Mikael Holmstrom, Lassi Luokkanen, Isak Hera-jarvi and Johan Santalahti gave the community its strong ethnic and cultural background. The village of Deep River (first called Forks) is located a few miles inland from the Columbia. It began as a logging community in the 1890s. At one time it, too, had its steamboat landing, stores, post office, school, and a hotel. With the abundant timber of the adjacent forest, streets and sidewalks were made of planks set on piles.

Deep River was probably one of the most isolated communities of the lower river. In his book, *Deep River*, author Carlton Appelo, a native of the community, says that people living there were accustomed to isolation because they had come from the fjords of the Scandinavian countries where people in neighboring valleys seldom made contact with each other.

The close-by community of Grays River, he writes, "a mere three miles by foot over trails which suffered from ample rainfall, was most conveniently reached by taking a boat to Astoria and then traveling back on the Grays River boat." It sometimes took two days to reach a town just a few miles from Deep River.

To open a road to the community, in 1928 Deep River residents hosted a benefit that must have been the social highlight of the area's history. Three steamboats from Portland and three from downriver brought some three thousand people to a picnic at a place called Svensen's pasture. The event raised $750 which was contributed to the construction of a road.

Appelo dedicated his book, *Deep River*, to his father, C. Arthur Appelo, who died there at the age of eighty-seven. In concluding his dedication to his father, Carlton Appelo writes:

Well, Papa – that is the Deep River story done the best I know how in the time I have available. I know your tale would have been more personal – sparkling with the incidents and humor which you alone could relate. That is not possible in this mortal world. When we next meet, you can set the record straight. I pray that I have done justice in telling of the tale.

It is signed, "Your loving son, Carlton."

Harrington Point

RETURNING FROM DEEP RIVER, I tried to close with the eastern side of Grays Bay. The lost community of Eden was located somewhere along that shore, but the water was too shallow for me to search for it. Coming around Harrington Point and regaining the main ship channel, I entered a different Columbia River. Below Harrington Point, the river reaches its greatest width. A broad expanse of water, nearly ten miles wide, lie between Grays Bay on the Washington shore and Cathlamet Bay on the Oregon shore. Above Harrington Point, low, sandy islands stretch out from the Oregon shore, and the main river channel is reduced to a width of less than a mile.

By certain definitions, Harrington Point is considered to be the actual river mouth. Downstream from the point, the river is considered an inland arm of the sea and it is salty on the flood tide. The real river begins above the point, above the reach of salt water.

In the early part of the nineteenth century, the location of the river's true mouth was an important issue. Great Britain argued that the United States' claim to the region drained by the Columbia was invalid because Gray's exploration was limited to the lower inland arm of the sea. Broughton, on the other hand, had gone upriver as far as the Sandy River, and therefore was able to establish the rightful claim to the river basin.

Altoona

WHAT IS LEFT OF ALTOONA straggles along a narrow shelf of the river shore just upstream from Harrington Point. It is a wonderful site for a village. The timbered hills rising above the town climb to a summit of a thousand feet. The location has a sweeping view of the wide lower river to the west, and to the south it looks out over the flat expanse of the river's green estuary islands.

Altoona orignally was called Hume's Station and acquired its present name from a boat. The boat was the cannery tender *Altoona* that owner Hans Petersen named for his hometown, the port city of Altona, Germany. In 1902, William Hume died and Peterson acquired the station. A store, warehouse, and lodging house were built at a cost of $2500, and in 1903, the Altoona Mercantile and Fish Company was formed. In 1904, a cannery (the Altoona Packing Company) and a boarding house were added to the growing community.

Unlike Frankfort and some of the other speculative land settlements of the lower river, Altoona was not founded on dreams for a future city. It had but one purpose, one life: fishing.

Though cut off from the larger world, Altoona was not immune to the effects of wars, financial panics, and social change. Altoona measured the impact of these events by the price of fish. Wars closed old markets and opened new ones. The opening of the Panama Canal changed the patterns of West Coast shipping. The age of sail ended and gillnet boats were equipped with gasoline engines. And around Altoona, roads and highways drew closer and closer. At first they were welcomed. The isolation of the community was lifted. With time, however, the roads and trucks that liberated the village killed it. Its slower way of life, tied to the main street of the river, could not survive a faster, more efficient pace. Born to the river, the community died when it became a part of the land.

The life of Helge Saari, Altoona's milkman for twenty-one years, reflected this theme. His dairy was located on the Crooked Creek estuary just a few miles from Altoona. As there were no roads, Helge made his milk deliveries by boat, a delivery schedule that had to coincide with the tide. Seven days a week, winter and summer alike, Helge would load a horse-drawn sled with milk, which he would drive across the shallow estuary to his waiting boat and then begin his deliveries. The chugging of his engine in fair weather or foul was the sound of Altoona's milkman. The construction of the road to Altoona in 1942 ended his business. A few months later he died.

Twice the little community made national headlines. On the calm Sunday evening of 28 May 1922, the American freighter *Iowan* rammed the British ship *Welsh Prince* in front of Altoona. Seven men were killed in the collision, and the rescued survivors were put ashore in Altoona.

Then, in 1930, a cold wave crippled the Northwest. Temperatures in normally mild Astoria dropped to twenty-one degrees and remained there for eleven days. The communities along the north shore were frozen in. Food supplies ran low, and cattle were in danger of starving. On 20 January, a low of fourteen degrees was recorded in Longview. Ice closed the river, and many river boats were frozen to their docks. Relief finally came to the communities when the lighthouse tender *Rose* was able to break a path through the river to deliver needed supplies to the ice-bound communities of Altoona, Pillar Rock, Brookfield, Skamokawa, and Cathlamet.

The last salmon in Altoona were canned in 1947. After that, the village no longer had a purpose. The tribute paid milkman Helge Saari on his death in a 1942 *Oregonian* editorial could also have served as the obituary for the community. "The man in question," said the article, referring to Saari, "has done nothing spectacular. He has just gone his weary way, filling his small niche in the scheme of things."

And so went Altoona.

Pillar Rock

PILLAR ROCK is a finger of conglomerate basalt standing twenty-five feet high, and one thousand feet south of the old shoreside community with the same name. A navigation marker, No. 17, lights the summit.

Indians called the rock *Taluaptea* after a chief who displeased the spirits and was turned to stone. Broughton named the rock on his upriver exploration of the Columbia in October of 1792. It was from a camp on the Washington shore, just opposite from Pillar Rock, that Capt. William Clark of the Lewis and Clark expedition wrote this stirring, but inaccurate log entry of 7 November 1805:

Great joy in camp we are in <u>view</u> of the <u>Ocian</u>...this great Pacific Octean which we been so long anxious to See. and the roreing or noise made by the waves brakeing on the rockey Shores...may be heard disti[n]ctly.

The entry was premature; the ocean cannot be seen from this shore. What was seen was the wide and stormy lower river, a difficult stretch of water that the expedition would spend the next ten days traveling through before reaching the ocean at Cape Disappointment.

A rain shower drove me to the shelter of the old Pillar Rock cannery for a cup of hot tea. Englishman John Temple Mason Harrington, the six-foot, 250-pound "Laird of Pillar Rock" opened this cannery in 1877 on the site of an old Hudson's Bay Company saltery.

Pillar Rock was even more deserted than Altoona. One white fishboat was tethered to its rickety dock. Grass sprouted from the tops of the line of pilings that lined its waterfront. The faded red cannery building stood empty under a rusting corrugated metal roof. Swallows darted in and out of the shed through the gaping holes and glassless windows of its time-streaked walls. A barely legible sign painted on the building carried the faded name "New England Fish Company." An old man with pants held up by a string wandered down to the dock.

"You're getting wet," I said as I offered him a cup of tea.

"Been wet all my life," he said, declining the tea. "Where you from?"

I explained that I was from upriver and that I was returning home. To this man, anyplace outside of Pillar Rock was the outside world, a place he remembered as other small communities like Pillar Rock. He used to "go out" he told me, to places like Skamokawa, Cathlamet, and Astoria. In each of these places he has an old fishing friend he assumes I should know just because I have been there.

"Been fishing sixty years," he told me. "Started when I was sixteen. Don't have a boat anymore so I don't get around so much."

He is one of the last of the old-timers of the lower river. He lived much of the history I was traveling to record. He still lives close to the docks, the net racks, the blue-stone tubs, and the boats that are the archaeological remains of an era that is past. Within his hands are the skills that made it all work, in his mind the memory of what it was like. But years and storms take their toll. Time for the last generation of boats, docks and fishermen is running out. We will not value these things – men or boats – until they disappear, until only written records and faded photographs are left.

There is yet time to save something. Deep River, Altoona, Pillar Rock . . . something of these places still exists. Each is an example of what a fishing community of the lower river was like. Something of them could be saved . . . if we cared.

From Pillar Rock, I continued my upstream trip along the north shore and tied to the rock wall of Jim Crow Point for lunch. The obvious racial connotation of the name is related to James D. Saules, a black man who served as a crewman aboard the Wilkes survey ship *Peacock*. After this ship was wrecked at the entrance to the Columbia, Saules remained in the area. For a while, he served as a bar pilot, put two ships on the river sand, and then settled down to running a freight boat from Astoria to Cathlamet.

Brookfield, situated behind the finger of Jim Crow Point, is no more. My morning's journey along the north shore had covered barely six miles. Of the seven little communities that once stood on this river shore, only two – Altoona and Pillar Rock – still stand. Brookfield is only an abandoned dock. Of the others – Eden, Catarddi, Carlson's Landing and Dahlia – nothing can be seen. They are gone forever.

Skamokawa

A GLACIER-LIKE FOG rolled down and out of the Skamokawa Valley and evaporated under the morning sun as it spread out across the river. Turning into the thick fog, I located the silted-in channel entrance to the little community that lies at the junction of three waterways, Skamokawa Creek, Brooks Slough, and Steamboat Slough. Years ago, these waterways were Skamokawa's main streets, and the town was called the "Venice of the lower Columbia." Sadly, the highway destroyed the orientation of the water-fronted town. Important buildings designed for river access were bypassed, and others were razed.

One such building – still standing, but badly in need of restoration – is Silverman's Emporium, built in 1911 as a general store, post office, and steamboat dock. As the fog cleared, I could see the tower of Skamokawa's old schoolhouse, which dominates the community from its hillside perch. Its louvered bell tower beneath a pyramidal roof vaguely resembles the architecture of the Queen Anne period. The school was dedicated 4 July 1894, with a community picnic and a traditional program of patriotic speakers. Children, living across Skamokawa's water streets, were rowed to the school in boats.

Skamokawa Creek flows under a highway bridge which opens on a massive gearing arrangement, now rusty with disuse.

Beyond the bridge a few old houses, built to face Skamokawa's main streets, still have their front doors facing the creek, and gardens that run down to the water's edge.

Cathlamet

FROM MY APPROACH BY WATER, Cathlamet retains the look of a traditional old river town. The town looks down from its hillside location to the weathered docks, sagging warehouses, sheds, and the old ferry slip clustered along its waterfront below. Low brick and wooden buildings face each other across the single downtown street, and other streets wander along the contours of the hill as though they were following routes laid down by old footpaths. These softer curves and lines give a pleasant and natural unity to the town. There are places where people work and places where people live, and both are tied to the presence of the river.

James Birnie, Hudson's Bay Company agent in the Columbia district, was the pioneer settler in Cathlamet. He moved from Astoria to Cathlamet in 1846 to operate a trading post for the company. The house built by James Birnie remains standing and is occupied by Julia Butler Hansen, a former congresswoman from southwestern Washington. Her grandfather purchased the house shortly after his arrival in Cathlamet in 1882. Julia Butler Hansen's grandchildren are the fifth generation of the family to sleep under the steep shingled roof of the old house and to play in its lovely garden.

By telephone, she consented to my request for a Sunday evening visit to her home. After greeting me, she led me to her living room where we sat surrounded by the memorabilia of her long and distinguished career in public service. She recalled for me the Cathlamet of her childhood.

Time, she said, was recorded by the arrival and departure of the river boats. Each arrival or departure was an event that drew people to the river to say goodbye or hello to a friend or a relative. Because of the isolation of the community, the steamboats were their contact with the outside world. They brought news, letters, freight, friends, and relatives to Cathlamet. In her childhood, she said, the anticipated trip was the annual down-river run to Astoria to visit the dentist and the shopping trip upriver to Portland. The old steamboats, said Mrs. Hansen, were a better public transportation system than Cathlamet has today.

For all of its isolation, she told me, Cathlamet had strong ties to the outside world through the diverse origins of its many ethnic groups. In addition to the Scandinavian families that centered on Puget Island, Mrs. Hansen remembers growing up with the languages and cultures of Indians, Sicilians, Belgians, Frenchmen, Italians, and Chinese.

Her memories of Cathlamet and its history were worked into a play she wrote and produced for the town's 1946 centennial celebration. She also served as costume designer for the play and laughed at the memory of converting old calico bedspreads stored in her attic into pioneer costumes.

She took me on a tour of the house, a place warm and bright with use and affection, and pointed out the organ shipped around the Horn, the display of old china, including huge platters mended with cleats of brass, desks of Civil War vintage, tea canisters from India, baskets woven by Indians, furniture brought overland on wagons, and chairs built by pioneer carpenters. This house and its contents are the history of a family, its traditions and its roots.

The treasure of the house is its art collection, the paintings of Maude Kimball Butler – Mrs. Hansen's mother – who, in her seventies, began a series of paintings of early Cathlamet, which she drew from memory. In the very best tradition of folk art, each painting relates a story of place and time, people and custom, landscape and building, craft and tool, pleasure and pastime.

The collection has been reproduced in a catalog issued by the Washington State Historical Society. Descriptive notes of each painting were written by Mrs. Hansen. In the combination of art and text, an evocative vignette emerges. Each picture portrays a piece of the life and time of a young Cathlamet girl from the 1880s to just after the turn of the century.

Yachts are the river traffic that visit Cathlamet today and its public marina at the opening of Elochoman Slough is a popular destination for lower river pleasure cruises. Harbormaster Vic Lawrence showed me through the marina and discussed the future of the town. Its history – like Astoria – might also be its future. Vic told me that the county is studying an overall economic development plan that calls for a program of historic preservation and the development of cottage industries and tourism. Back in his office overlooking the marina, he gave me a copy of the study and told me that a public meeting had been scheduled that evening to present the plan.

Twenty or so people were already gathered in the local grange hall by the time I got to the meeting. They were patiently listening to a young man from the Cowlitz-Wahkiakum Governmental Conference present the details of the development plan. A long list of improvements is proposed for the area, which includes the two communities of Cathlamet and Skamokawa.

Proposals for the improvement of Cathlamet included such projects as brick sidewalks, cobblestone streets, underground wiring, old-fashioned streetlamps and benches, downtown storefront improvements using historical design themes, restoration of the steamer dock, a waterfront park, and a commercial fishing museum. For Skamokawa, proposed improvements included restoration of the old schoolhouse, a net loft, and the development of a gillnet fishboat exhibit.

Questions of doubt punctuated the speaker's presentation. The comprehensive plan would be costly. The audience was mostly elderly, and skeptical, and conservative. The staff speaker understood that and proceeded cautiously. He also knew that they had seen their children forced to move away from the two communities because of the area's high rate of unemployment. His mission was to give credibility to the idea that the area could – by mutual determination and effort – lift itself from economic malaise. And before the evening meeting was concluded, he had gained support for the plan.

Mrs. Everett Groves came forward to announce that she and her retired husband were already planning to open their home on Puget Island as a bed and breakfast inn. Irene Martin, librarian at the tiny, one-room Skamokawa library, said that she had just finished a personal twelve-year project; a history of Skamokawa. Steve McClain described the vintage 1913 gillnet boat he and a group of volunteers were restoring. The meeting broke up in a babble of conversation, for hope had replaced skepticism.

Puget Island

BERGSENG...Hegstad...Kaukkanen...Ostervold...my fingers ran down through the columns of names in the telephone directory for Puget Island. It read like an outpost of Scandinavia. I was looking for the number of Marvel Blix, a boat builder who lived somewhere on the island. I called the number from Cathlamet, but it was busy, so I decided to chance a visit in my boat, hoping that he would be at home.

Marvel Blix, I was told when I asked for directions to his home, lived on the other side of the island, "Over by Welcome Slough. Can't miss it."

I rounded the lower tip of Puget Island and then headed up along its southern shore to Welcome Slough, a little community built along the diked edge of an inlet which dead-ends in the center of the island. Small frame houses painted in bright colors face each other along the narrow tree-lined slough. Green lawns, flowers, hanging glass floats, stacks of cut firewood, and the steeple of a clean-lined, white church competed for photographs as I motored slowly past docks, sheds and moored boats.

But no Marvel Blix. His shop, I was told, is on the main river, just upstream from Welcome Slough. I found him standing in the shop doorway, just looking out at the river. After an exchange of greetings, he invited me in to the shop for a look around. It is a clutter of lumber, tools, power machinery, engine parts, paint cans, timbers, barrels, rope, and everything else that looks and smells like boats.

Marvel Blix is a soft spoken man, probably in his sixties, and very neatly dressed. He told me he was building his "last boat." It is to be a twenty-two-foot sailboat built on the lines of a small Norwegian cod-fishing boat. He showed me the half-model he had carved to develop its lines. The use of the half-model is an old way to design a boat. It was the method used by boat builders before the modern methods of marine design were developed. The boat was conceived in a block of wood, carved, and worked to the shape of a boat. The proof of the vessel's lines lay in the eye of the model maker and the feel of his finger tracing out the planes water would follow past the bow, under the turn of the bilge, and outward under the stern. The wall of the boat shop was a display of half-models, warm, varnished sculptures of wood that portrayed the evolution of gillnet boats from sail to gas engines.

The models represented the designs and boats of three generations of Blix family boat builders. The senior Blix, Marvel's father, had just died at the age of ninety-six. Marvel started building boats when a completed gillnet fishboat sold for $165. The last gillnet boat he built was in 1978. It sold for $34,000.

Stacked by the door of the shop were large planks of cedar he was drying for the new boat. They were of a width and thickness I had never seen, and I asked him where he had bought them.

"Didn't buy them," he said. "River washed them up on the beach."

The eruption of Mt. St. Helens, and the flooding that followed along the Toutle and Cowlitz rivers had uprooted a red cedar tree, five feet wide at its base and some forty feet long. The Columbia then carried the log downstream and left it high and dry on the beach in front of Marvel Blix's boatshop. So far, the log had produced enough planks for three boats, with enough left over to plank a Norwegion cod-fishing boat.

Marvel Blix has never built anything except wooden boats. As he sees it, referring to the use of fiberglass construction materials, "A boat shouldn't come in a five-gallon can."

Prairie Channel Villages

AT PUGET ISLAND, I was forty miles inland from the mouth of the river and had completed the northern half of my journey along the lower river shoreline. From the island, I crossed over to the Oregon shore and headed back downriver through the backwaters of Prairie Channel.

With the exception of a few local fishboats and an occasional tug pulling a raft of logs, Prairie Channel is seldom used. The name was easy for me to understand because parts of it reminded me of an endless prairie of waving green grass brightened by yellow flowers sprinkled by the wind.

A few small communities along Prairie Channel still hold to the river edge out of habit and tradition. These communities on the Oregon shore, like other settlements on the Washington shore, had no future after they ran out of what the world wanted from them – fish and lumber. What is left can only be reached by boat or dead-end roads, and visiting them is like taking a short journey backwards into yesteryear.

Bradwood is located on the main river just above the opening of Clifton Channel. A tiny inlet off Clifton Channel led me to the stillness of an old millpond where I tied up the boat. Walking towards the nearly deserted town, I crossed through a field of tall grass. Its golden cover hid rusting cables, wheels, gears, and assorted machinery left behind when the large Bradwood sawmill was closed and dismantled.

Bradwood was a company-owned milltown. Residents were all employees of the mill who lived with their families in company-owned houses and shopped at the company-owned store. I wandered undisturbed with sketch book and camera down the length of Bradwood's one dead-end street – quiet, tree-shaded, and deserted. There was not much to record: one old gas pump, a weathered door, and a broken window that framed the interior of the abandoned community store. Left undisturbed, I thought, Bradwood in a hundred years might be an important archaeological site for a later generation curious about an early twentieth-century milltown.

Clifton

MANY OF THE OLDER COMMUNITIES along the lower river were settled by tightly knit ethnic groups. Finns, Norwegians, and Swedes were the dominating influences of many of these tiny communities. Clifton, at the upper end of Clifton Channel, was settled by descendants of Mediterranean stock – Greeks, Yugoslavs, and Italians.

Andrew and Katie Marincovich were the last and only full-time residents of Clifton when I visited them in their neatly kept, white house which looks out on the river. Andrew and Katie were both born in Clifton. Andrew, spry and well into his seventies, poured me a half-glass of whiskey as I sat at his breakfast table Sunday morning. He said he couldn't imagine a better place to live. Once he tried another place – California – but he didn't like it. He will never leave Clifton again, he said, until, "I go out feet first." He remembers the old community of Clifton as though it was only yesterday.

"We had two saloons then," he said, refilling both our glasses. "A saloon and a dance hall in the lower part of the town and another saloon in 'Greek town'." Each year, he added, the town imported a boxcar of grapes which the community pressed for wine.

Clifton's population began to decline in the early 1920s, the aftermath of an Oregon law that made it illegal for persons who were not American citizens to commercially fish. The older people – immigrants – had to leave and try their hands at new jobs. Clifton, like Altoona, was never anything but a fishing village.

Andrew stayed on. He had been in charge of the Bumble Bee Company's fish station at Clifton. A few years ago, the company decided to sell the old dock and the fish station it owned at Clifton. Nine old-time residents of the community bought the dock just to save the old facility. Andrew bought the old *Duke*, the boat he operated for the company. He keeps the *Duke* tied to the dock in front of his house. Like the old-timer in Pillar Rock, Andrew, the old fishing dock, and the *Duke* – all three are the very last of their kind.

A strong headwind slowed my downriver progress, and at sunset I pulled into a dock at Aldrich Point a few miles downstream from Clifton. It wasn't long before I had a visitor. He was Albert Smith, son of a family that for generations had been fishermen and boat builders on Block Island off the coast of New

England. He had come to the shores of the Columbia, bringing with him the traditions of East Coast boat design, which he recreates in the elegant lines of the Swamscott dories he builds in his one-man shop.

All along the river I met young men like Albert Smith. Some worked on tug boats, others fished. For all of them, the hours were long, the work hard and the pay marginal. Money does not seem to be their motive. Rather, it is an independent kind of life that appeals to them, a life that is somehow bound up with the river and the old occupations it still makes possible.

Through them, some of the crafts, the skills and the traditions of the river are kept alive. By word, I attempt to describe the history of the river. By hand and deed, they keep it alive.

Grizzly Slough, Gnat Creek, Marsh Island, Brush Island, Blind Slough were some of the names of places I passed as I continued downstream through Prairie Channel. Each name probably commemorates nothing more significant than an animal seen, an infestation of insects, the vegetation of an island, and a dead-end backwater. But what of the islands called Minaker, Quinn, and Tronson? Who were these individuals who left their names along that shore? Who and why?

Svensen

SVENSEN WAS THE LAST COMMUNITY I visited on my journey along the forgotten lower shores of the river. It is an island, a few fishboats, some gray weathered houseboats with flowered window boxes, and a bridge that connects it to the mainland. The bridge rises from the opposite shore in a gentle arc, crosses a narrow inlet of water, and ends in a farmyard. Quite by accident, the bridge is one of those rare structures in which the opposing forces of tension and compression seem to be visually balanced in harmony.

I stood at the high center of the bridge and just stared at the water below. It is an occupation of the sunny hours for fishermen, old men, and itinerant river philosophers. The tide goes out, the tide comes in, and sometimes a boat passes under the bridge.

I imagined, looking out from the bridge, what it might have looked like at dusk many years ago when Svensen's fleet of gillnet boats put out for the nightly drifts, and then returned before dawn under the pinpoint of their running lights to pass, at the end of the long fishing night, beneath the dark shape of the bridge. It is a scene that will never happen again.

Two things are different about Svensen. It is supposedly the only community in Oregon that ever voted for the Commu-

nist Party. Its radical politics were, perhaps, the legacy of rene-
gade Peter Svensen, who jumped ship in Astoria and settled in
the area in 1877. The second thing is that its name is spelled
differently from the "Svenson" on the Washington side of the
river.

Cemeteries are quiet; so are nearly abandoned villages. Both are
places to contemplate time and the transience of things human.
In the short journey I made around the shoreline of the lower
Columbia River, I passed the sites of twenty-eight communities,
some still trying, but most of them gone. That sets a record of a
dead or dying community for every three miles I traveled.

Today, such a loss of human communities would probably be considered as a social disaster. The little villages of the
lower river did not exist in an era of social concern. No one –
outside of the villagers themselves – really cared whether they
lived or died. Quietly without fanfare they came into existence,
and quietly without eulogy they disappeared.

Cut off from the world, their societies demanded hard
work and a high degree of self-dependence. Their unwritten social code was the culmination of mutually acceptable rules that
were enforced by habit, tradition, and necessity. It is doubtful
that they cared too much for the world that ignored them. They
were the last of the river frontier. Remarkably, many of them
hung on as late as World War II when the changing conditions
beyond their riverbank were finally too sweeping for their way
of life to survive.

Wallicut, Stringtown, McGowan, Chinookville, Point
Ellice, and Megler, Knappton, Frankfort, Oneida, Deep River,
and Eden, Catarddi, Altoona, Carlson's Landing, and Dahlia,
Pillar Rock, Brookfield, Svensen, Clifton, and Bradwood . . . all
of these places are now only names in history, a part of the river
we will never know.

Islands of the river

Estuary. The word has a kind of wave-like rhythm when it is pronounced. It comes from the Latin word *aestus* meaning a "heaving or surging motion." An estuary is that concluding part of a river in which the currents of the river are affected by the ocean's tides.

Consider its connections. A distant sun powers the system of the earth's weather. It draws water from the sea, vaporizes it and spreads it over the land as rain or snow. Streams gather the water and form rivers that return the water to the sea under the pull of gravity. As the water moves, currents wash the river bed and disturb its substances. Rocks grind on rocks. Sand is formed. It travels with the river for a century of centuries and comes to rest on a sandbar when it encounters the opposing current of the ocean's tide. Other grains are trapped. A sandbar emerges from the river's surface. A seed is trapped. It roots and grows. In the shelter it creates, sand blown by the wind is caught. An island is formed, an island of the estuary.

Twice in each twenty-four hours the island's shores and low places are a part of the land. Twice in each twenty-four hours they are reclaimed by the river as ocean tides fill the estuary, block the river current, and raise the level of the water.

Aestus. Estuary. In the chemistry of water and sunlight mixed by the tide, life on this planet was formed. The process continues. The estuarine system is the world's most productive life source.

The Columbia River estuary islands form a chain that begins just above Tongue Point and follows the Oregon side of the main channel upriver to Tenasillahe Island. The area is designated as the Lewis and Clark National Wildlife Refuge and thirty-five thousand acres of open water and tidelands are contained within the system. Twenty-odd islands and hundreds of mudflats, bars, and tidal marshes form a land area of ninety-four hundred acres.

The area is uninhabited by humans. The only structures in the area are a few houseboats, a fallen-down barn in an island cow pasture, and one or two navigation aids that mark the twisting channels. Two small communities, Svensen and Clifton, are the only settlements along the shore. Except for these few alterations, the natural appearance of the estuary islands is unchanged.

Dawn of the Estuary

ON THE BRIGHT MORNING of a day that had no fixed objective and no schedule to keep, I began my exploration of the estuary chain. I followed the ship channel along Astoria's waterfront, past anchored ships that dwarfed my boat beneath their rusting sides. At Tongue Point, I turned out of the main channel and entered shallow Cathlamet Bay. It is the threshold of a different river. Broad, flat and slow moving, it seemed to emerge from a backdrop of low, green marshes.

Stiff-legged herons too numerous to count stood at the edges of exposed mudbanks and white patches of seagulls clustered on the narrow fingered sand spits. I passed islands with names of "Green," "Grass," and "Marsh" that formed wide, green fields of waving grass.

The engine was turning at slow speed. The wash of my propeller scoured the shallow river bottom and stirred its mud to leave behind me a trailing line of churned, brown water. I did not need a tide table to tell me it was nearly low tide. With an oar, I probed for the bottom. Water depth, including muck, just covered the blade. For my boat there was no danger. Its shallow draft, scoop bow, and pivoting outboard engine were designed for shallow river travel and for grounding without damage.

A small channel that had cut its way through grass-topped island banks opened in front of me. Though very small and unnamed, the chart showed that if I was able to cross its shallow outfall, it would lead me into an interior maze of veined waterways that drained the island. It was worth a try.

With the engine shut off, I poled my way slowly into the narrow lead. It formed a nearly waterless ditch that flowed between twin banks of sun-glazed mud. I felt like some aquatic rat or mole slithering through a hidden trench below the waterline of the earth, which hovered above me as a line of green grass. Looking up, I could see the exposed roots of the grass, an interwoven fabric of dense strands that formed a tight band of living stitchery at the top of the mud-banked moat.

The boat came to a gentle stop in the clinging suction of the mud under its bottom. There was no retreat; the sea had pulled the water out from under me with the falling tide and closed the downriver opening of the channel. There was nothing I could do but to await its return. I felt just the slightest apprehension that high water might not return, that I might be stuck forever in the hot, windless mud world that has lost its cover of water. Nothing stirred. I could almost hear the sound of drying mud. For the estuary and its sleeping life, it was the midnight time of low tide.

My eyelids grew heavy and closed. Waking, nothing seemed to have changed, but something had. There was the faintest pulse of life returning. Small noises bubbled and popped around me as though the skin of the earth was stretching and tightening. My eyes closed and then opened again. Noiselessly, imperceptibly, the water had risen and crept back over the sun-baked mud. Napping, gazing, listening, waiting, I watched the slow rise of the estuary dawn. A floating bit of grass drifted towards my boat and was pinned by an invisible current against its transom. Again I dozed off, this time to be awakened by the feel of the boat bumping along the mud-edged channel. There was an itching, buzzing feeling to the heat, and a strong smell of rich dampness, pressing and claustrophobic.

With relief, I found that there was enough water under

my boat for me to continue the passage. With a pole I pushed my way ahead. The water continued to rise. I could not see it happening, I could only see that it had. From the blindness of the trench bottom, I had been lifted to where I could look out across broad fields of grass which rippled in wave patterns with the running wind. The air was fresh, moving, and alive. The channels, brimfull, reflected the blue sky and white clouds as they separated and then merged again to form islands within islands. The earth had sunk, the water had risen; I had seen the dawn of the estuary.

I could only imagine the orgy of death and the feast of life for the millions of creatures that occupied mud, sand, nook, hole, shell, and burrow beneath the water in the drowned world of high tide. With mouth, claw, tentacle, and filter they were each eating what the current delivered, or were moving with it to be eaten. In the flood of mixing waters, salt with fresh, the sun was at work with the raw material of life, using the cells of dead matter to feed living forms. Through the alchemy of the estuary, life was being created, and I was privileged to have spent the morning in its genesis.

Drama of the Estuary

THE DRAMA OF THE ESTUARY is not easy to see nor is it fully understood. It is even difficult to offer a comprehensive definition of an estuary. The Columbia River estuary is a good example of this ambivalence. It is affected by the tide strongly enough to have the currents that flow through the islands change direction with each run of the tide. Yet the Columbia system lacks a primary ingredient of the classical estuarine system – the intrusion of salt water in any significant amount. The huge volume of fresh water carried by the Columbia postpones any significant mixing of fresh and salt water except at the extreme lower mouth of the river. Therefore, the entire system above Tongue Point is more accurately described as a freshwater tidal marsh. Even that description is somewhat contradictory, because fresh water is not normally tidal without significant salt water intrusion.

The estuarine system, therefore, is best understood as a concept rather than as an exact geographic location. Its complexities are enormous, its secrets are within the closely held mysteries of river currents, tidal influences, and the energy of the sun which is converted through chemistry to life.

River currents and the deposition of silt or sand particles are easily understood. In the hydrology of a river, silt and sediments drop to the bottom when the river current slows. River currents are slowed by such things as curves in the water course, islands, obstacles in the river, and shallow areas.

Millions of tons of sediment are carried downstream each year by the Columbia. The overall load has been substantially reduced by the more than 130 dams built in the Columbia River drainage basin. These dams block the transport of water sediments and reduce the scouring action of river currents. Even so, the river still transports a heavy load of earth. In the narrow river section of Beaver Point, fifty miles upriver from the river mouth, a U.S. geological survey recently estimated an annual sediment load of 7.5 million tons of transported materials. This material is the construction resource of island building.

In some ways, the overall appearance of the estuary or salt marsh system is rather monotonous. Its waters are less influenced by the effects of wind and wave because of the protected enclosures formed by mudbanks and island barriers. Currents are more sluggish because of the physical obstruction of the islands which retard river flow. Shorelines consist of drab mudbanks topped by tangled brush thickets or flatgrass marshes. Only a few islands have sandy beaches that invite one to step ashore. In most places, a foot meets the squishy resistance of a water-soaked bog. But the visual aspect of the estuarine system – though at times and in places haunting and lovely – is its least important dimension. The apparent placidity of the estuarine system covers a multidimensional environment that is turbulent with life, never fully at rest, and constantly in flux as sea dominates river and is, in turn, dominated by river.

Life in the estuary, if it is to survive, must be capable of adapting to one of the world's most unstable environments. Change is the only constant in the estuary. Many of its life forms exist in a transitional zone between fresh and salt water. Other physical and biological systems of the estuary are neither freshwater or salt, nor are they transitional. These forms are uniquely adapted to the estuarine system and thrive on its complex variability.

Various life forms tend towards specific zones selected according to their particular requirements for water composition, temperature, type of bottom or clinging surface, oxygen content, and other life requirements. They share with each other one common characteristic, the ability to survive and adjust to a constantly changing environment.

The mechanisms for life survival in the estuary environment are amazing. Some forms survive through sheer productivity of breeding. Many have developed structural systems that allow retreat into shells to avoid unfavorable conditions. Others burrow or dig, and still others are capable of crawling or swimming to stay within tolerable margins of acceptable conditions.

The survival of the entire estuary environment is based on the interrelationships of its many separate parts. Shallow areas slow currents to trap silt which renews the structures of shores and mudbanks after the erosion caused by spring floods.

The floods themselves infuse the water with new oxygen supplies after the dormancy of winter's lower water stages. Sunlight is trapped during the process of photosynthesis and is converted to fuel for plant life. Plants decay and become food for diatoms and plankton, which in turn feed fish and shellfish. Birds feed on these larger forms and deposit their excrement, which furnishes needed nutrients to plants, which decay . . . and so on in the never ending circle of estuarine life.

Much of the life of the estuary is microscopic and exists between tiny particles of sediment. Others form film-like colonies on rocks, plants, and wooden pilings. Their numbers are staggering. Amphipods, small crustaceans that build tube-like burrows, have been found in the Columbia River in densities of fifty-seven thousand per square meter. Oligochaetes, a class of annelid worms, have been found in concentrations as high as seventy-five thousand to the square meter.

Our minds cannot comprehend such abundance. We are also slightly repulsed by the snapping, sucking, squirting dark terror and anarchy that crawls, wiggles and burrows in the muck of mud and in the green ooze of water. It is here that the food chain begins, but our aesthetic preference is for creatures a few steps up the ladder. Birds, for instance, which emerged from the sea, but left the land for the air.

Of marine birds, wading birds, shore birds, game birds, and raptors, 175 species have been identified in the Columbia River estuary system. The isolation of the islands – meaning distance from human interference – is one of the attractions that draw such a large bird population to the area. Diversity of habitat is another reason.

The wading birds – great blue herons, gulls, sandpipers, and plovers – wade the extensive sandbars and mudflats of the river channels, and stalk the miles of shoreline in search of small fish, water insects, worms, and crustaceans.

Other waterfowl use the protected shallows of the islands for resting, feeding, and breeding. During the fall and winter seasons, these wild birds gather in great flocks to feed in the tidal marshes before they begin their migrations south.

The multitiered heights of this vegetation – the low-waving stalk of the salt marsh grass, the intermediate height of the willow and the tops of the cottonwood and fir trees – provide nesting sites and lookout perches for many small birds such as the fast flying swift, the darting kingfishers, and the calling blackbirds.

A number of bald eagles nest in the taller trees that grow on the higher land areas above flood levels. In addition to the more common raptors such as owls, hawks, and the osprey, the rare peregrine falcon and the snowy owl have been observed in the estuary.

An inventory of the estuary's abundance is almost limitless. Mice, weasel, vole, shrew, rabbit, squirrel, and chipmunk inhabit the island forests and thickets, there to be preyed upon by raccoon, opossum, coyote, skunk and fox. Fur-bearing animals of the aquatic habitat include beaver, river otter, mink, muskrat, and nutria. Fifty rare Columbia White-tailed Deer live in the protected preserve of the Columbia White-tailed Deer National Wildlife Refuge on Tenasillahe Island. Additional herds of this endangered species live in another section of the preserve on the Washington shore.

Diked, filled, and paved, old estuaries are the sites of many of the great coastal cities of the world. In our exploitation of the Columbia River, we have ignored the chain of estuary islands simply because we have not devised a means of converting their resources to profit. Now preserved, they will remain a river wilderness.

In 1977, CREST prepared an inventory of both the physical and biological characteristics of the estuary. The inventory has served as the basis in the development of a comprehensive land and water use plan for the lower river. The inventory of the islands provides its own conclusions: The estuary is an essential and integral part of the river and effective planning should leave it untouched.

I make no pretense as a scientist. My observations of the estuary were made as I wandered through its green-lined channels or tied up to the roots of a willow tree during a long summer evening to watch its slow quiet life. I have gone to the islands in the fall to watch the winged flights of geese and swans that stir the air with wing beat and call. I go not to hunt, but to gather my trophies with eye and ear. And once, deliberately, I went out in my boat to confront the first storm of the year blowing in from the Pacific. I tied the boat to the shore of a tiny grass-rimmed inlet and laid there in silence as the storm howled over me, creating a wild ocean of waving grass. I go there as a visitor and leave behind only the quiet wake of my boat. It is a place to be visited, to be seen. And to be left alone.

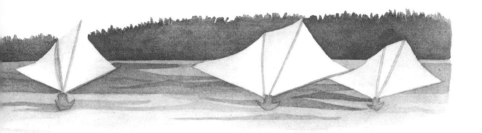

Fishermen of the river

Aʙᴏᴠᴇ ᴘᴜɢᴇᴛ ɪꜱʟᴀɴᴅ, the Washington shore rises to a steep cliff above the river's edge. Cape Horn, lifting to over twelve hundred feet, is a dominating point which forces the river to curve around its palisaded shore. A short distance upriver from the cape, the cliffs fall back to form a steep-walled amphitheater floored by a dry cover of rocky land. I landed there at the place called Eagle Cliff to visit the site where, in 1866, the first salmon cannery on the river was built. Nothing remains of that important structure, nor does any plaque or memorial indicate that from this location grew the leading industry of the lower river.

The Columbia River fishing industry was one of the world's last fishing areas to be developed. On the East Coast, the fishing banks off New England and Newfoundland had been fished since the early seventeenth century. Portugal was one of the leading nations to utilize the fisheries of the New World. Its boats and methods evolved from the centuries-old fishing techniques used in the waters of the Mediterranean. The Columbia River had no fishing tradition (except for its native tribes) and, beginning late, had the advantage of being able to adapt the well developed technologies of other fishing industries to its special requirements.

In 1820, the Hudson's Bay Company in Astoria packed salted salmon in barrels, and exported two shipments to London where it arrived in an inedible state. The first successful export of salmon was made by Captain John Dominis. In the summers of 1829 and 1830, he anchored his ship *Owyhee* off Deer Island and packed fifty barrels of salmon, which he sold in Boston for ten cents a pound.

By 1835, the Hudson's Bay Company, then located at Fort Vancouver, was annually shipping three to four thousand barrels of salted or pickled salmon to the Hawaiian Islands.

The pickling or salt method of preserving salmon was not very successful. Production was limited because of a constant shortage of both barrels and salt. A larger problem was the fish itself. The flesh of the salmon is rich and oily. It did not take to the salt cure method which was successfully used by the New England cod fishing industry. During the French Revolution, Napoleon offered a prize of twelve thousand francs to any person who could develop a method of food preservation for shipboard use. Nicholas Appert won the prize in 1809 by developing the process of cooking and sealing the food in airtight glass jars.

This was the technology that was needed to make an industry of the Columbia River salmon resources.

The process quickly reached the United States where it was improved by the use of tin cans instead of glass jars. Delaware oysters were among the first seafoods to be preserved by the new canning process. The potential of the new technology was quickly noted by the Maine fishing firm of Hapgood, Hume and Company. By the time gold was discovered in California, the firm had perfected the canning method and was looking for new areas of expansion for its fish canning business.

The company relocated on the Sacramento River in California and found a ready market for its first two thousand cases of canned salmon, which were packed behind a shielding curtain so that no one could copy the process. It was a short-lived enterprise. Hydraulic mining destroyed the salmon habitat for spawning, and the company again went looking for a new river to fish.

Hapgood and the Hume brothers – George, William, Joseph, and Robert – came north to the Columbia River in 1865 and located at Eagle Cliff. They brought with them a knowledge of canning and a fishing boat that revolutionized the old native way of fishing from the river shore with spruce-root nets.

At the Sacramento River operation, the Hume brothers had fished with small skiffs. Scouting for a larger boat, they had visited the boat-building firm of Griffin and Cooper in San Francisco. The yard had just completed an open, double-ended rowing and sailing boat for a customer known only as "Greek Joe." The Humes ordered a copy of Greek Joe's boat and took it with them to the Columbia after they closed their Sacramento cannery. From this boat evolved the craft still known as the Columbia River gillnet boat.

During their first winter at Eagle Cliff, Hapgood and the four Hume brothers hand-cut cans and mended nets for the spring fishing season. In the first year of operation, 1866, four thousand cases of salmon were packed. The company met with immediate success. By 1873, each of the Hume brothers had his own cannery. By 1879, seventeen canneries were operating along the lower river. By 1883, the number of canning operations had grown to thirty-nine. In that year, the canneries packed 629,400 cases of prime Chinook salmon. That year's production – only seventeen years after the beginning of the industry – was a production record that has never been exceeded.

Anyone or any group able to scrape together enough capital for a boat, a net, and canning equipment could try his luck. The Hume brothers made fortunes, and so did many others. But as more and more canneries were built, the competition for fish and markets resulted in higher prices paid to fishermen and lower selling prices for the canned product. The industry was forced to develop technical, organizational, and marketing innovations. Each new technique or strategy that developed was quickly copied, and then became an industry standard.

In some respects, the industry developed certain processes and equipment that were remarkably similar to the later mass-production methods of the automobile industry. The gill-net boat is an example.

The basic design of the Hume boat was improved by the chance visit of Joshua Slocum (later to achieve fame for his first solo circumnavigation of the world) to Astoria where he tried his hand at fishing. Slocum built a larger boat which measured twenty-five feet long, had a six-foot beam and a draft of two feet, six inches. He decked over the boat's bow and stern, added low washboards, a sprit rig, and a centerboard. As this boat evolved, a second sail was added to the single mast. Running homeward before the fresh westerlies, the twin-sail boats looked like butterflies and became known as the "butterfly fleet."

The design quickly became the standard for the industry. Since all fishermen fished the same waters in the same conditions, and sold to more or less common markets, one boat type met the requirements of all the fishermen. Building methods and materials became standardized, thus lowering the individual cost of each boat. Another factor that lowered the time, labor, and material cost of each boat was that the great majority of them were purchased by the canneries and rented to the individual fishermen. This allowed orders for boats to be placed in advance, therefore materials could be purchased in larger quantities at substantial savings. Permanent jigs for construction could be set up by boat builders, and patterns could be made for parts separately cut prior to assembly to further the economics of a semi-mass-production system.

Nets, corks, oars, sails, and other items of equipment were likewise standard throughout the industry, thereby making equipment more readily available, and at a lower cost per unit. In later years, the standard Columbia River fishbox that was used for transporting fish foreshadowed the sophisticated materials-handling methods of modern industry. These boxes, all following a standard rule of width, length, and depth, could be stacked in uniform loads of weight and measurement.

The Hume brothers were among the best of the innovators. R.D. Hume was the first to acquire a modern machine for soldering cans, another device to seam the cans, and a later machine that automatically filled the cans. Remembering the demise of the salmon in the Sacramento River, Hume developed the first commercial salmon hatchery on the river and took an early lead in attempting to convince state and federal resource managers about the value of commercially raised salmon fingerlings.

It was also R.D. Hume who developed a foreign market for Columbia River salmon. Between 1900 and 1915, sixty percent of the pack was exported to Great Britain to provide an inexpensive food for Midlands industrial workers.

George Hume first employed Chinese laborers as cannery workers around 1872. Chinese immigrants performed the labor intensive task of cleaning and preparing salmon for the can. Open immigration laws allowed large numbers of Chinese to enter the United States where they were employed at very low wages. Because the canneries were a seasonal industry, these Chinese workers drifted back and forth between Seattle, Portland, and San Francisco, and were brought to the lower river canneries as contract labor. The system was a terrible exploitation of the Chinese workers, but it did provide the canneries with a dependable labor force. This phase of hand labor was eliminated around 1905 with the introduction of a machine known as the "Iron Chink," which soon replaced the Chinese workers.

Around 1900, a gasoline engine was developed that could be used in a gillnet boat. The engine quickly replaced sail power. As larger engines became available, the design of the gillnet boat changed, and eventually the double-ended boat gave way to the more popular square "tunnel" stern boat that could support a more powerful engine.

By 1915, the gillnet fleet – by then all gas powered – numbered 2,856 boats. Over three hundred fishtraps were working the lower Washington shore off Chinook Point and in Baker Bay. More than fifty horse-drawn seine nets worked the shallows of the beaches and the midriver sandbars. The combination of gillnet boats, fishtraps, and seine nets presented a formidable obstacle to fish entering the river.

Commercial fishing in the lower Columbia was a hard, rough, and sometimes dangerous profession. Most gillnetting was done at night when the net was invisible to the salmon. Fishing continued in all kinds of weather short of actual storms. As the boats had no sheltering cabins, nights were long and cold.

Many fishermen drowned each year. In just one storm on the night of 3 May 1880, twenty men perished. The best fishing was near the mouth of the river. The practice was for boats to run down towards the bar on an outgoing tide and return on the flood. Often boats were carried to sea where sudden storms would catch them in the exposed waters beyond the bar.

A study of fishermen incomes for 1883 shows that the average gross income per boat was $808.00. One-third of that amount went to the cannery for the rental of the boat and gear, leaving a net income of $268.50 for each of the two-man crew.

The season lasted only four months to give each man an income of only $67.00 per month during the fishing season.

Canneries extended credit to the fishermen for the purchase of food and supplies at cannery-owned stores. The credit system created a bond of debt between fisherman and cannery company that had advantages and disadvantages for each. The fisherman owing money was assured of getting a boat from the cannery in order to pay off his debt. However, in exchange for the privilege of credit, he was paid less for his fish. The cannery, by extending credit, could anticipate a more stable source of fish, but was obligated to tie up large amounts of capital in non-productive loans.

The immigrant Chinese were not allowed to fish the river. The law that kept them off the river was the determination of the Occidental fishermen to keep the river for themselves. This law was enforced by the power of the vigilante. This story appeared in an early 1880s article in the San Francisco *Chronicle*.

Some years ago a few adventurous Mongolians joined the fleet. They disappeared the same night. Their boats were broken to pieces and their nets cut up and scattered on the beach. The fishermen made no attempt to conceal the fact they had drowned the intruders.

Of the estimated twenty-five hundred fishermen of the period, only thirteen percent listed the United States as their birthplace. Most of the fishermen were from the Scandinavian countries, with Sweden listed most often as place of birth followed by Norway, Finland, and Denmark in that order. Other ethnic groups included Greeks and Yugoslavians. The boarding houses of Astoria were home to many, and Astor Street – called "the most wicked place on earth for its population" – was their playland.

As early as 1875, fishermen made an unsuccessful attempt to organize themselves along the lines of a trade union. Success came in 1886 with the formation of the Columbia River Fishermen's Protective Union. The union immediately increased the selling price of fish from fifty-five to sixty-five cents a fish. By 1888, canneries were forced to pay $1.25 per fish, and the union was recognized as a force to deal with by cannery owners.

Cannery companies began to construct their own fish traps in order to gain direct access to the supply of salmon. Most of these traps were located near Chinook Point. Fishermen claimed that the traps interfered with their fishing because they presented obstacles to their drifting nets. When gillnetters attempted to pull the piles on which the traps were hung, federal troops were called in to restore order. These traps were a major issue in the long and bitter strike of 1896, which lasted three months before a compromise was negotiated. Although both sides claimed a victory, it was the union that lost in the long run because the cannery owners banded together in an organization known as the Columbia River Packers' Association. The association permitted cannery owners to cooperate in presenting organized resistance to union demands. In addition, the association absorbed a number of canneries in an effort to stabilize production and began developing cooperative marketing strategies.

The common threat, of course, was the slow decline in the numbers of fish returning each year to the Columbia. The industry was aware of this decline, and as early as 1908 attempted to have legislation passed that would outlaw fishwheels on the upper river. The subsequent legislative battle was not based on a philosophy of conservation but, rather, was a battle between two competing segments of the industry for the harvesting of the available salmon.

Today's fights between offshore trollers, sport fishermen, gillnetters, and native Indian tribes is a continuation of the same fight. The contest is to determine which group has the right to catch the last fish.

Village of my twelfth summer

From EAGLE CLIFF, I backtracked to the time, years ago, when I spent my twelfth summer with a boyhood friend in a small, roadless fishing village on the lower river shore. It was just prior to World War II, and the little community existed as a part of the traditional fishing industry I described in the previous chapters. I consider myself fortunate to have lived and worked in that village because the experience permitted me to be a part of a community and a way of life that no longer exists. I remember that wonderful summer in a village of enchantment, now gone, but locked forever in my memory.

We arrived on the little steamer that made daily freight and passenger runs from Astoria, two boys, alone, on their first summer away from home. Homesickness was cured with my first view of the village. I had arrived in adventureland.

The village was only a line of unpainted wooden houses built back from the beach. A planked sidewalk, built over wooden pilings, angled from one house to the other, tying the community together in a walkway that ended at the large fish dock and steamer landing which was the village center. A large red fish house was at one end of the dock. On the other end, fishnets were strung out over the bare poles of mending racks. Beneath the dock, the green and gray hulls of the fishboats were tied to pilings at bow and stern.

We were met at the dock by my friend's grandmother, who lived in the village. She was the picture of what a grandmother should look like: thin, gray hair tied in a bun, faded floral dress, gold-rimmed glasses, and a flour-dusted apron tied around her slim waist.

Her house was as neat as a pin and she ruled it with mop and broom. We were given the rules: Keep out of the kitchen except at meal time. Stay out of the parlor at all times. Wash on the backporch and keep the woodbox filled.

For a bedroom, we were given the hayloft over the barn. It was, she said, "Good enough for boys." It was better than good enough; it was perfect. We slept in the hay under a covering of old deer skins. We hung all of our clothes on two nails in the wall. There were no beds to make, no floors to sweep and nothing to pick up. And there was plenty of company: bats overhead, mice in the straw, and cows and chickens below.

I vividly remember awakening to the dawn in that loft. The animals below made the first stirrings; soft clucking noises of the hens, the discordant crowing of the roosters, and the rubbing sounds of cows scraping their shoulders against the barn stalls. The sun would glance through the cracks in the barn wall, a grid of light that patterned the yellow hay of the loft and turned to gold the specks of dust that rose from our straw bed when we got up.

Early mornings were cold by the river. Colder yet was the wash water in the gray enamel pan on the backporch. It was a naked run from the barn to the wash basin and then to the warmth of the woodstove in the kitchen.

A few days after our arrival, the grandmother said to us, "Tonight you will go with Fred in the boat to fish." The village elders had decided that Fred would be our instructor in the ways of fishing, and that was the end of the matter. From then on, we went out gillnetting nearly every night with old Fred. With the net out, we would drift, and Fred would instruct us in the two other subjects besides fishing he believed important for boys to know – sex and swearing.

Sex education was presented in the form of lusty ballads that Fred sang to us as we waited to pull in the nets. The finer points he elaborated on with details of his mythical exploits in Astoria's red light district. It was a wonderful introduction to the facts of life, a ridiculous presentation of human biology and function that we thought hilarious.

Swearing was a part of the job. Along with the vocabulary of profanity – some in English, most in Finnish – came the rules for its use: Never in the house and *never* in front of the grandmother.

And so the hours of the first drift would pass and the sun would drop over the edge of the sea at the distant line of the river mouth. Sometimes a moon would light up the river, sometimes the night would be utterly black with only the tiny light from the float at the end of our net line twinkling in the dark. Then Fred would start to haul in the net by hand. Our job was to pull at the long sweep that would hold the boat position perpendicular to the net. And then with Fred heaving and swearing and one of us at the sweep, the magic would begin as the great, gleaming salmon were pulled from the dark river and thrown into the fish well where we stood with bare feet. Up to our ankles and then to our knees they would pile as we slid and slithered in a welter of blood and slime, still keeping to the pull of the oar.

Sometime after midnight we would lay out the second drift. Then we would sleep, curled up in the bottom of the empty net well without a blanket, while Fred kept watch over us singing to himself. During the second haul in the cold, dark hours before dawn, my friend and I would fight for the sweep to have something to do to keep warm.

Loaded, we would cross the river to Astoria and unload our night's catch at the fish buyer's dock. Then, with money in his pocket, Fred would leave us in charge of the boat while he made his morning rounds of the Astor Street saloons. We were forbidden to follow because, said Fred, "Astor Street is not for boys."

Fred would be gone an hour or so, and when he returned, he would make his way none too steadily down the ladder that led to the boat. He would then fall asleep and our glory hour would begin: We were left in command of the boat, and our job was to run it back across the river to home. We had to lay a course that would clear the sandbanks, the seine nets, and the ferry crossing, round the point, and run the boat into its moorage. There had been no formal instruction as to how to do this. We had seen Fred do it, and it was expected that we would know how when the time came for us to run the boat. I think we were the last generation of boys to be trained by the village to be fishermen. It did not last out another one.

Back in the village with our work over, there were infinite possibilities for the day. Like Indians, we gathered wild berries from bushes, apples from the trees, and licorice root from the moss of the forest. With old fishboxes, we built rafts and floated the river, ran naked along the beaches, and swam in the small creek behind the house. The grandmother, busy about the house with canning, cleaning, and sewing, left us alone. We were expected to be nothing but boys, by her definition half savage, dirty, and always hungry.

World War II came. I grew up but I never forgot the village. On my trip upriver, I decided to stop and see what had become of the old place. Dense woods came down to the shore where I beached my boat. The old dock was gone, and there was no sign of a house or a person. The only sounds were the cries of the crows and the gulls. I located the creek that had run by the house and followed it through the brush to the little clearing where the house had stood. Nothing remained but a pile of boards all fallen in a tumble. Atop this pile grew hundreds of daffodils, bright yellow in the morning sun.

Like Brigadoon, my village had disappeared. I sat among the daffodils and nearly cried. Not out of sadness that it was gone, but because it was all still there in my mind, the memory of my twelfth summer in a small fishing village on the shore of the Columbia.

In that memory I see a time of bright silence and a small fishboat crossing the path of a setting sun. An old man stands at the wheel, and next to him, two boys sit at the stern of the boat with bare feet hanging over the side, swinging to the easy motion of the boat's passage through the waves.

Gull Island

Two weeks on the river and I was only fifty miles upstream. My wake, had it been recorded, would have revealed a slow, wandering track of curiosity – islands explored, old townsites discovered, and unnamed channels followed. I had left footprints on sandbars, and on mudbanks I had left the imprint of the boat's keel. These things, the small unexpected adventures, are the best part of a journey. From Eagle Cliff, I went to look for new adventures away from the main channel of the river and found a pencil-thin waterway bisecting Wallace Island which had to be explored.

The mouth of the channel was obstructed by sunken logs and low hanging branches. Entering it, I passed from the open river into a channel that led me along a watery path through a tangled forest of cottonwood trees. From time to time I had to clear the channel of logs that blocked the way. It was only a short voyage across the island to its other side. The boat emerged with a few more scratches and its decks littered with twigs, but I had gained the pleasure of knowing that I had gone where few boats had ever traveled . In my time, a man can't discover a river, but he can always be on the lookout for an unexplored ditch.

Another diversion lay ahead. Beaver Slough runs like a squiggly worm across the land, twisting and turning away from the main river to reach the small town of Clatskanie a few miles inland. I passed through a green waterway that led me past farms, staring cows, and under a bridge to a town just opening for the day.

To me, the great pleasure of water travel is the landfall. It mattered not that I had only followed a slough to a small farming town. Coming from the water, it was still a foreign city, though I explored it no further than its closest breakfast cafe.

I returned to the main river at Oak Point where the river narrows to less than a half-mile wide. It was probably the narrowness of the river corridor in this area that prompted Nathan Winship and his brothers – Abiel and Jonathan – aboard the ship *Albatross*, to attempt the first settlement on the Northwest Coast here in 1810, a year before the founding of Fort Astor.

The Winship brothers were looking for furs. They built a fort on the Oregon shore and planted a garden to feed their settlement. What they failed to consider in the selection of their site was the spring flood of the Columbia, which, when it rose, destroyed the fort and covered the garden with two feet of water. Although the Winship brothers settled at Oak Point on the Oregon shore, somehow the name crossed the river to the Washington shore where it is located today.

Above Oak Point, the river contains between its shores Crims Island, Gull Island, and Bradbury Slough in a topography of shore, channel, and islands that is a classical profile of river formations. River sand is the construction material and current is the architect. Sand and current, together, shape the river forms of channel, shallow areas, shore, islands, and sandbars.

An experienced river pilot would not need a chart to find his way through this area. Understanding the river forces at work, he would be able to "read" the river by observing visible conditions that would reveal to him the depth and contour of the unseen river bottom.

All the conditions of river channeling and island building are particularly visible in the area of Crims Island. Upriver from the narrow channel at Oak Point, the river current slows. The first law of river hydrology says that when a river current slows, the sediments it carries drop to the river bottom. Crims and Gull islands, in the slowed backwaters of the river above Oak Point, have been formed because of this physical law. The river then directs its energies to the task of cutting through the obstacles it has itself formed, and creates the tiny, thread-like channels that I explored on my circumnavigation of Crims and Gull islands.

In these channels, miniatures of the river's large, main channels, I played at being a river pilot and guided the boat through them by closely reading and interpreting the design of the river.

River water is pulled everywhere by an equal force of gravity, but the distance around the outside of the curve ahead of me was greater than the distance around the inside of the curve. The water, like the rim of a wheel, traveled around its outside circle faster than it did around its inside corner. The faster moving water on the outside curve scoured out a natural channel, which I followed, while the sediments picked up by this scouring action were dropped in the slower currents to form the obstacles of shallows, sandbars, and islands.

Correctly, I read the river and followed its small channels around Crims Island, only to ground on the hidden sandbar that formed the long downriver tip of Gull Island. But it was time to stop, the island was deserted, and I went ashore to explore it for the rest of the day.

Of all the world's geographical forms, I find islands the most pleasing. They seem to offer the possibility of an adventure of some sort just because an island is somehow distant and different from the mainland. An island is a law unto itself, a suspension of other laws. An island is a place for outlaws, misfits, hermits, poachers, and fellow escapists. An island like Gull Island, small enough to walk around, yet large enough to hold some secrets, allows an expression of the solitary Crusoe that is within me. It provides a geography of solitude that I can enjoy without ever feeling lonely. All that was needed was a driftwood shack.

In a sand clearing just back from the river edge, I started to build one. I selected the root and stump of a tree left at some long ago high water mark as the starting structure for the shelter. Then I went hunting along the beach to scavenge for building materials. With a shelter in mind, the worthless debris of a beach becomes valuable building material. I found planks, boards, boxes, an old door, and a glassless window frame. Instead of carrying them, I threw them back into the river and floated them to the site of the shack. (Ingenious are the enforced skills of building without tools or nails.) By evening I had what I thought was a unique shelter, and I moved in for the night. The various boards and planks formed shelves and seats, and the door a table. The shack was memorable because of its view. The glassless window propped up in the sand framed the river and an evening sunset. Without a ceiling, I had over me a canopy of stars, a soft night breeze and the first light of a fiery dawn. In the morning, I disassembled it and carried its parts back down to the beach for the river to float away and left Gull Island.

Visions and settlements

THE FINGERED PLUMES of smoke from the Longview mills hung over the river in a dense cloud. Passing under the high span of the Longview Bridge, I left behind the undeveloped lower river shores and started through an industrial glut. On one side were the Longview mills, on the other shore, the machinery, tracks and rusting equipment strewn on Rainier beach.

Behind Longview's belching stacks, its wall of water-front buildings and a jumbled skyline of pipes, conveyor belts, ventilators and flashing lights lies an outdated dream of urban aesthetics, the planned city.

When Long–Bell Lumber Company president Robert Long chose the old townsite of Monticello on the Columbia River for his company's new mill, he aimed to build something better than "just another mill town." Longview, one of the world's largest post-industrial planned cities – was the result of that ambition.

When his southern mills began to run out of timber in 1919, Long was faced with the choice of going out of business or going west. He elected to move, and in 1921 acquired his first timber holdings in Cowlitz County, and three thousand acres on the Columbia as a site for a mill. The new city was the next project. Long purchased all the land that lay between the Cowlitz and Columbia rivers, and had it diked, graded, and leveled. By 1922, forty-four miles of streets and seventeen miles of sidewalk had been constructed. The city was essentially completed by 1927, but it did not reach its full development until the World War II period.

Today, Longview has outgrown its central plan, but what Long did build has survived, and though it is now surrounded by very ordinary strip developments, it remains a pleasant reminder of one man's dream for something better than "just another mill town."

In contrast to the Longview mills, the towering, sculptured shape of the Trojan nuclear plant's cooling tower a few miles upriver from the city is almost lovely. No hissing valves, clanking chains, or conveyor belts mar the symmetry of its hourglass shape of molded concrete.

Lovely, proportional, and eerie, with no one to be seen about its premises as I passed under its plume of steam, a feathery cloud silent and white. Perhaps the Indians who buried their dead there were prophetic. The place is called Coffin Rock.

Kalama, just upriver from the Trojan nuclear plant tower,

once boasted that it was located "Where Rail Meets Sail." It was the booster slogan that was to lift the fortunes of the settlement by making it the seaport and rail terminal of the Columbia. Kalama's hopes were built around the Northern Pacific Railroad which tied the community to Tacoma and Puget Sound. The southern end of the line terminated at Kalama and began again at Goble on the Oregon shore. Freight cars were carried across the river on the 338-foot ferry *Tacoma*, which bridged the rail system. The ferry was first built in New York, then it was taken apart and shipped around the horn in fifty-seven thousand pieces and reassembled. Kalama's hopes for river supremacy were destroyed when a new railroad cut a direct line over the Cascade Mountains to Puget Sound and bypassed the community.

One of my favorite river pioneers, Ezra Meeker, was an early Kalama settler. Meeker came overland to Oregon by ox wagon in 1852. In 1916 he made the same crossing by car, and he then lived long enough to cross the continent again by airplane in 1924.

On 20 January 1853, Meeker wrote in his book *Pioneer Reminiscences*, "I drove my first stake for a claim, to include the site where the town, or city, of Kalama now stands and here built our first cabin."

He continued:

That cabin I can see in my mind as vividly as I could the first day after it was finished. It was the first home I ever owned. What a thrill of joy that name brought to us. Home. It was our home, and no one could say aye, yes, or no, as to what we should do. No more rough talk on ship board or at the table; no more restrictions if we wished to be a little closer together . . . We had been married nearly two years, yet this was really our first abiding place. All others had been merely way stations on the march westward from Indianapolis to this cabin.

The spring flood that year on the Columbia sent a great number of logs floating down the river, which Meeker gathered together to form a raft. Setting out downriver with the raft, he intended to sell the logs at a sawmill at Oak Point. The current, however, carried the raft past Oak Point and, he wrote, "to Astoria where we sold them for eight dollars instead of six per thousand, thus profiting by our misfortunes."

Summarizing pioneer river life, Meeker wrote:

I can truly say that of all those years of camp and cabin life, I do not look upon them as years of hardship. To be sure, our food was plain as well as dress, our hours of labor long and labor frequently severe, and that the pioneers appeared rough and uncouth, yet underlying all this, there ran a vein of good cheer, of hopefulness, of the intense interest always engendered with strife to overcome difficulties where one is the employer as well as the employed. We never watched for the sun to go down, or for the seven o'clock whistle, or for the boss to quicken our steps, for the days were always too short, and interest in our work unabated.

Late in the afternoon I reached St. Helens. From the river, the dominant feature is the clocktower which tops the stone courthouse. When the courthouse was built in 1906, St. Helens was an important river town with mills, shipyards, and a steamer landing lining its riverbank.

All of that is gone now, and St. Helens has become two towns: old St. Helens facing the river with its rather drab mainstreet, and the St. Helens along the highway strip with its franchised restaurant chains and shopping centers. But the old town with its river setting might yet turn out to be the city's real treasure. Some forty-seven acres of the downtown area has been declared a National Historic District. With a little paint, the removal of some cosmetic storefronts, and some landscaping, the old city with its courthouse square could become a showplace of the river.

St. Helens was founded in 1847 by H.M. Knighton, who laid plans for what he believed would be the main port of the Columbia. Many other communities were in the same contest. Oregon City had been founded by the falls of the Willamette River, and its promoters hoped that the power of the falls on a main tributary river of the Columbia would make it a major port and industrial city. Two others, Asa Lovejoy and Francis Pettygrove, had flipped a coin that selected the name Portland for a new city they hoped would be the winner.

Knighton figured to outfox all rivals by locating his city at what he believed would prove to be the head of ship navigation on the Columbia. Old river charts show that Knighton made a logical choice for the site of his city. Just upstream from St. Helens, an extensive sandbar blocked the natural river channel. This bar was formed by the entering currents of Multnomah Channel, the Lewis River, and Lake River. Nature, Knighton figured, had provided him with a renewable condition that would assure the success of St. Helens.

What he failed to consider was the plan of the U.S. Army Corps of Engineers that called for the blasting away of Warrior Rock just upstream from St. Helens on the tip of Sauvie Island. By eliminating a large section of the point, the river cut a natural channel through the sandbar that ships could follow to gain the upper reaches of the river. St. Helens, like Astoria, sat helplessly as ships passed upriver to the growing town of Portland.

Crossing the Multnomah Channel, I rounded the sharp point of Warrior Rock and ran close along the wooded shore of Sauvie Island. Sediments dropped by the entering Willamette River formed this island, the largest island of the Columbia River.

Somewhere on the island lie the ruins of Fort William. Built by Nathaniel Wyeth in 1834, it was the second American outpost in the Northwest. By then, Fort Astor had been abandoned and the Hudson's Bay Company had moved its headquarters to Fort Vancouver. Wyeth's plan was to challenge the company's domination of the region with his own fishing, farming, and fur company. In 1832, he started west from St. Louis with a company of forty men. Desertions along the way seriously reduced his party's strength, and when he arrived at Fort Vancouver nearly destitute in October of the same year, he was forced to return immediately to St. Louis. On his second attempt, Wyeth sent his ship, the *May Dacre*, ahead of his expedition with the intention that it would begin his Columbia River fishing operations. Again, misfortune plagued Wyeth. The ship arrived too late to begin fishing operations. The Sandwich Islanders he had imported to work at Fort William deserted, and in June 1836, Wyeth abandoned Fort William. Two men from his party remained behind, Calvin Tibbetts and Solomon Smith. They became the first and original American citizen-settlers of the Oregon country.

Sauvie Island today is the rich farmland of Wyeth's vision. The island itself is formed by the collection of river silts and alluvial deposits at the confluence of the Columbia and Willamette rivers. Multnomah Channel separates the island from the Oregon shore. The island beaches fronting the Columbia River are the summer playground for hundreds of sun-seeking Portland residents.

Strict zoning laws have wisely preserved the island's rural landscape. Vast wetlands and lake areas in the island's interior are owned and managed by the Oregon Fish and Wildlife Commission, and these ponds are the feeding, breeding and resting sites for millions of ducks and geese who pass over the island on their annual southern flights.

On Sauvie Island, in a field now overgrown and a barn now fallen down, I once helped construct a large wooden schooner. I remember driving down a roadway that tunneled through overgrown blackberry bushes to reach a clearing in which the sagging, time-tired barn stood. Rusting farm machinery lay about the barnyard, nearly covered by golden hay gone wild. The hundreds of swallows that had taken over the barn would dart and dip through the air and then land in little clearings of dust where they would preen and smooth their feathers.

Countless times I parked the car and then stepped into the shadowed space of the barn. Its open north wall, like a huge skylight, admitted the strong sunlight, and the distant view of Mt. St. Helens, untouched by volcanic activity, with its rounded dome bared of snow.

Across the road from the barn was my great outdoor clock; the open fields of the island. In the spring, when I began to work on the boat, the fields were carpeted with green shoots of new hay. Later, the full grown hay of midsummer swayed in the wind like a green ocean around the barn. And then, as the seasons moved one into the other, the fields were mowed, and the hay was baled and left behind to dry in the sun as cubes of tawny gold scattered over the ground. By these fields, I measured time and the slow work of building the boat.

My hands also marked the passing of time. When I began work on the boat, they were soft, white, and tender. With time, they became etched with the black lines of pine tar and rough with calluses where skin pressed against the knob of the plane, and the handles of hammer, chisel, and saw. My hands were alive with fingers and skin singing of their usefulness.

Slowly, boards became planks, cut and trimmed to a size that became a part of the boat. Cut and plane, fit and spike. The fields turned from green to golden yellow and then to bare ground under clouds of winter gray. Time itself was building the boat. Time was also measured in the growth rings of the wood that went into the boat: Oak that was a living tree when Lewis and Clark camped on the island and that might have provided shade for the Hudson's Bay cows that grazed there in 1838.

Two ships heading downriver pressed me close to Sauvie Island as they rounded Belle Vue Point where the Willamette River joins the Columbia. I waited for a tug pushing a train of barges to enter the Willamette, and then I crossed over to Kelley Point and anchored for lunch just below the ships loading and unloading at the sprawling Port of Portland marine terminal.

Oregon's first land promoter, Hall J. Kelley, would have enjoyed that view of this busy marine thoroughfare. Kelley (for whom the point is named) was a Boston schoolteacher. Acting in response to what he believed to be a divine inspiration, Kelley organized the American Society for Encouraging the Settlement of the Oregon Territory, the basis of which was his evangelical philosophies of civil and religious freedom. With circulars and speeches, Kelley gathered support to colonize a country he had never seen but believed should be settled as part of God's plan for a new promised land.

Kelley made the trip to the territory, and arrived sick and destitute at Fort Vancouver with only the tattered remains of the loyal band that set out with him from Boston. He returned to Boston and continued to preach and write about the virtues of the "new Eden" until his death at the age of eighty-five.

William Clark was the first white man to visit the Willamette River and the future site of the city of Portland. On the journey down the Columbia, the expedition had missed the mouth of the Willamette River, which lay hidden behind islands. An 1876 Corps of Engineers map of the mouth of the river shows these islands – Coon Island, Nigger Tom Island, and Percy's Island – as they existed before river improvements altered the natural river mouth. On the return trip upriver, the extensive valley lying between the Coast Range and the Cascades was noted and geographical logic suggested that a river had to exist to drain the valley. From Indians of the area, a sketch was drawn of the river they called the Multnomah, and on 3 April 1806, Clark explored the lower reach of the river.

From its mouth he was able to see Mt. Hood and Mt. St. Helens (previously named by George Vancouver) and Mt. Jefferson, named by the expedition for the then president of the United States. Although white men had not yet traveled the Willamette, Clark found that their disease of smallpox had preceded him and had already killed a large number of the river area Indians.

Preferring the back channels of the river over the main shipping channel, I continued up river along the south shore of Hayden Island through an American-style Venice. The houseboats, docks, and boats of a floating village crowded both shores. Many of the floats which support the houseboats were covered with green carpets which, from the river, made them appear as if they were floating on green lawns. The lines of parked boats were silent and deserted that Monday workday morning that I traveled past the rows of river residences. It was the boat names that interested me, fantasies of freedom and macho-sexism expressed in such names as *Foxy Lady, Whispering Wind, West Wind, Wet Dream, Day Dream, Hot Spur, Traveler, Scot Free, Revenge, Time Chaser,* and *Sounds of Silence.*

Other names – names that no longer exist – also intrigued me. Hayden Island (a rather drab name) was named after Guy Hayden, who acquired most of the island in 1850. His name replaced two other, older names given to the island, one or the other of which I think should be returned.

William Broughton named the island "Menzies Island" after Archibald Menzies, botanist on the George Vancouver expedition. Among the many northwest plants and trees recorded by Menzies was the fir, *Pseudotsuga taxifolia,* later called Douglas-fir. The Oregon economy was founded on this tree, but the name Menzies does not appear anywhere on an Oregon map. On second thought, the island would be a poor namesake for Menzies. There are few – if any – fir trees on the island because most of the island is now covered with shopping centers, parking lots, and condominiums.

The second name was bestowed on the island by Lewis and Clark. Noting an elaborately carved canoe with a high, ornate stem beached on the shore, the island was given the rather poetic name of "Image Canoe Island."

I think of the Interstate Bridge as the dividing line between upriver and downriver. The influence of the Pacific has largely diminished. At Astoria, the range of the tide is over six feet. At Vancouver, it is less than two feet. Below the bridge, I think of where the river is going. Above the bridge, I think about its source. Mt. Hood straddled the river ahead of me as I left Hayden Island, its foothills blocking the river's horizon to the east. These hills form the threshold to a river linked not to the tidal movements of the sea, but to the rhythms of ice and snow.

The upper reaches of the Columbia travel through a vast

region that is semiarid, cold in winter and hot in summer. Moisture that feeds the river falls largely as winter snow which accumulates on millions of acres of mountains and high plateaus. Winter stays late in these regions and spring, when it does come, quickly melts the winter snowpack which is carried by thousands of rapidly rising tributaries to feed the gathering force of the river.

Unlike rivers of the western Cascade slopes which flood in winter under the runoff of heavy rain, the natural flow of the Columbia is lowest in the winter season because its water sources are trapped in the form of snow. In the spring, when the rains diminish, other rivers drop. It is then that the Columbia rises to its full strength. It is sometimes a river of havoc.

Two years, 1894 and 1948, stand out as records. River flow is measured in terms of cubic feet per second (cfs.). In 1894, the flow was estimated at 1.2 million cfs. In 1948, the year in which floodwaters destroyed the war defense housing city of Vanport, the river reached a flow of one million cfs., though the flood was somewhat moderated by upstream dams. By comparison, the mighty Missouri – a legendary trouble maker – has never exceeded a flood flow of seven hundred thousand cfs.

According to the river flow charts maintained in Vancouver, Washington, by the Corps of Engineers, I was traveling the river during the August period of low stream flow, around two hundred thousand cfs. Such a measurement in a small boat with a ten horsepower outboard engine is meaningless. I converted cubic feet per second to something I could understand – buckets – and figured that each second, my engine was laboring with all its power to push me upstream through two hundred thousand buckets of water pouring down the western slope of the continent.

Deepwater ships rarely pass upriver beyond Vancouver. Because of limited river depth and width, Vancouver was and is the head of ocean ship navigation on the Columbia. For that reason, the Hudson's Bay Company selected this site in 1825 for its headquarters, Fort Vancouver. It was a double gateway site. To the west, the river gave the fort access to the sea. From that direction it received supplies and sent out its wealth of furs. Eastward lay the tributary streams of the Columbia, and from the valleys of those tributary streams came the beaver and other fur-bearing animals that were the source of the company's wealth. The area controlled by the fort extended from the Pacific Ocean eastward to the Rocky Mountains to take in most of what now comprises the states of Oregon, Washington, Idaho, parts of Wyoming and Montana, and large sections of British Columbia.

I crossed to the Washington shore, parked the boat on a sandflat, and hiked up to where an authentic reconstruction of the palisaded fort has been built. All of the trades and crafts that were necessary to sustain the many needs of the outpost empire are exhibited in the historic reconstruction – blacksmiths, wheelrights, carpenters, coopers, and others. The display of these craft industries and the extensive gardens and orchards that have been replanted around the fort, show that Fort Vancouver was no crude outpost, but a largely self-sustaining community and an efficient administrative center for a commercial empire larger than all England.

It was too big, too successful, and the site was vulnerable to invasion, not by sea, but by land. The Columbia River provided the only water route through the high Cascade Mountains. A canoe loaded with furs could come down the river and through the mountain barrier. And so could a man with a family and a wagon on a raft. All up and down the East Coast, along the Mississippi and in the South there was the spreading lure of something called "Oregon." It rekindled the quest that was the objective of so many of mankind's migrations. Out there, it was said, was free land for farming.

An outline of a road to the area called Oregon had been described to the U.S. Secretary of War in 1830 by the mountain man, Jedediah Smith. He described the ease by which wagons and stock had already reached the eastern slopes of the Rocky Mountains. Benjamin Louis Eulalie de Bonneville, a U.S. Army officer, was given the task of extending the wagon route through the Rockies to the Green River, which lay on the western side of the divide. The gateway to Oregon stood open.

First a trickle, then in straggling groups, and then by the hundreds they came, floating down the Columbia from The Dalles to arrive exhausted and near starvation at the doorway of the fort. Dr. John McLoughlin, Hudson's Bay Company's chief factor at Fort Vancouver, took them in, fed them, resupplied them, and sent them on their way. They crossed the river and settled in the broad and fertile Willamette Valley. It was not long before the British flag that had welcomed them at the end of their long journey stood as a nagging reminder of history. Their views had clashed with the British in 1776 and again in 1812. Monarchy and royal charter could not coexist with the brawling, lusty independence of a New World frontier. The battle was not fought again. The Hudson's Bay Company withdrew from Fort Vancouver, and the American flag was flown over their surrendered empire.

The last steamboat

THE HUDSON'S BAY COMPANY owned the first steamboat on the
river, the *Beaver*. Built in England, the *Beaver* sailed around Cape
Horn and arrived at Fort Vancouver in 1836. But Dr. John
McLoughlin, chief factor at the fort, would have nothing to do
with the new vessel and sent it north where it ended its days at
the Hudson's Bay post of Fort Nisqually on Puget Sound.

In 1850, Astoria launched the first steamboat to be built on the river. Appropriately, it was named *Columbia*. The ship began regular passenger and freight service between Astoria and Oregon City, and the run was an immediate success.

The second steamboat on the river was the *Lot Whitcomb*, built and launched in Milwaukie. Its captain was John Ainsworth; the chief engineer was Jacob Kamn. These two men, with partners Simeon Reed and R.R. Thompson, later formed the Oregon Steam Navigation Company. This company soon dominated the river with its fleet of steamboats, which served the growing cities and industries of the entire Columbia River system until the railroads ended the steamboat era.

The old sternwheeler, *Georgie Burton*, made the last run. She had seen a lot of history between the time of her launching in San Francisco in 1906 (the day of the great quake) and that blustery March day in 1947 when she headed out on her last trip. The *Georgie Burton* was going into retirement as a museum in The Dalles. I wasn't there to go with her. The experience I had gained as a deckboy on the *Burton* had earned for me the job of an able-bodied seaman on a World War II freighter, and in the spring of that year I was somewhere in the North Atlantic.

For a year the *Burton* remained docked and idle in The Dalles. Then the river called her back. In that record flood of 1948, the old sternwheeler slipped her moorings and was carried downstream where she was destroyed.

When I worked aboard the *Burton* as a fifteen-year-old deckboy, the boat was hauling log rafts from Blind Slough near Astoria to the Crown Zellerbach pulp mill at Camas. My deckboy's job was on the foredeck of the steamer where I worked the winches that tightened the cables that bound the logs together in rafts for the upriver tow.

I was totally inexperienced, and I was hired at such a young age only because of the war-time shortage of manpower. The complexity of levers, clutches, and brakes that I was supposed to use to control the large steam-driven winches completely baffled me. The spinning drums and whipping cable ends made my job a dance just to stay alive.

But worse than my fear of death was my absolute terror of the captain who controlled the operation by voice command from the lofty wheelhouse above my head. He did not order me about, he whipped me with verbal curses. For twelve hours a day I would work on that deck beneath his all-seeing view, and tremble under his curses while silent tears washed down my grease-smeared cheeks. Nothing I could do was right for him. Wrong lever, wrong timing, wrong kid for the job. Yet in spite of the agony of my poor bruised, cut, and cursed body, I felt no anger or resentment for that man. On the contrary, I thought him godlike, and I only wanted to be a good deckboy under his command.

My workday on the river began at 6:00 A.M. and ended at 6:00 P.M. Right after dinner I would go to my tiny cabin and fall asleep. Around eight I would be awakened by the mate.

"Cap wants you in the wheelhouse," he would tell me. It was not an invitation; it was an order.

Half asleep and limping, I would climb the long ladder to the pilot house, step inside, and, without a word, sit down. For long minutes "Cap" would say nothing as he stood behind the varnished roundness of the great spoked wheel and scanned the river ahead. I would just sit there watching the green walls of the river shores pass by. And then:

"See that patch of water over there?"

I would leap to the window to stare in the direction of his gaze.

"See how the water looks a little different? Sandbar under there."

That would be all. No explanation, no elaboration. Observation followed by conclusion.

"See that tug? Watch how he works his barge into the dock."

"See that white snag on the shore. Remember it. It's where you have to start making your turn."

My turn? Yes, my turn. He was telling me what someday I should have to know if I wanted to stay on the river. I could begin on the foredeck, and if I could survive the work and the abuse, I could watch as a student in the wheelhouse. Process and education were all one thing. I wanted to survive; and learn. I had visions of myself in Cap's hat.

I have never forgotten the soft, quiet hours of those summer evenings in the pilot house of the old *Georgie Burton* where the hidden secrets and the unwritten knowledge of its pilot were revealed to my youthful mind. I was convinced that I sat in the starboard seat of wisdom and I was learning.

But not fast enough. Next morning, I was the stupid deckboy again, the little sonofabitch who didn't know a peavy from a teaspoon, and who would lose his way inside a funnel. It was another day of tears and hopeless trying through long hours of shame, pain, and humiliation.

Then one day it stopped. Nothing was said. I was not much better at my job, but I had survived the ranting, cursing, whipping anger of the captain and I had not crumpled. My apprenticeship of fire had been served, and in recognition of that I was given my own boat to command. It was the *Burton*'s leaky old skiff.

"Mate," said the captain, "launch that boat overside with that kid in it. I'm sick of looking at him."

With that command and a push over the side I landed in the skiff with its sails flying. The skiff was untied from the moving sternwheeler and I was given the simple choice of learning to sail or swim. Somehow I was able to clear the thrashing paddle wheel at the steamer's stern, survive its monstrous wake, trim the sails, and return to the side of the moving vessel. Hands reached down to welcome aboard the *Burton*'s deckboy, the humble title I earned in an era of the river that ended with my youth.

To the reach of the tide

JUST EAST OF TROUTDALE, I entered the gateway to the Columbia Gorge. It begins as a sharp rise of hills on the east bank of the
Sandy River. The flat, eastern edge of Portland pushes to the
very edge of the hills with its sprawling housing tracts and industrial parks, and then, abruptly, the city stops and the gorge
begins.

Lieutenant William Broughton, sent by Vancouver to explore the Columbia, was the first man to look into the depths of the gorge. Broughton landed in a longboat just east of the Sandy River, and on the moonlit night of 30 October 1792, claimed all the land of the Columbia watershed for Great Britain.

Thirteen years later the Lewis and Clark expedition emerged from the gorge after an eighteen-day canoe voyage down the Columbia. Dates and figures give no drama to what I consider must have been one of the great small boat voyages of history. West of Walulla Gap, the river is bounded by the high walls of the gorge. The downriver voyage is an ascending drama of geological violence. The old river traversed by the expedition was a series of rapids and currents which carried them through the deepening gorge to the climatic cut through the spine of the Cascade Mountains. These men were from the relatively low and gentle lands of the eastern United States. What, I wondered as I looked upriver into the gorge, were their thoughts and anxieties as the river currents and rapids carried them downstream through a formidable gorge of unknown dangers to an unknown destination.

I could wonder about the human side of the Lewis and Clark expedition because I, too, was in a boat on the river about to enter the gorge. From my level on the water surface, the river disappears, and mountains stood across my path. The rim of the gorge rises to three thousand feet, and to nearly five thousand feet at its highest point. These summits are not distant peaks set back at a distance from the river; they are the sidewalls of the gorge itself, the vertical shoreline of the Columbia. From river edge to mountain summit is one great leap.

The rising westerly winds were my concern as I entered the gorge. Like a funnel, the gorge admits the westerly winds which gather along the barrier of the Cascade Mountains and accelerates their velocity as they blow through it. Page 244 of the *U.S. Coast Pilot* states that here:

*the river flows between bold mountains of the Cascade Range. In this
stretch, winds of considerable force prevail during much of the time; gener-
ally they blow upstream in summer and downstream in winter. Daily
peak velocities vary from 6 to 42 knots, but Corps of Engineers officials at
Bonneville Dam measured gusts as high as 76 knots.*

Off Corbett Station, it began to get a bit bumpy. At Tunnel Point, it was blowing hard. I made for a sheltered inlet and
tied up for the night behind Rooster Rock, the cleansed name of
the phallic-shaped rock the pioneers called "Cock Rock."

The next morning at dawn, on the last day of my voyage,
I greeted the lifting summer sun as I traveled beneath the steep
cliffs of Cape Horn in a deep corridor of retreating night. When
the sun topped the hills and touched the river, the gorge flamed
into a canyon of light that shadowed the isolated pinnacles and
promontories rising like castled buttresses above the river.

It is hard to realize that water could do this to stone, I
thought as I stopped and touched my hand to the river, soft, wet,
and cool. The currents took command of the boat, and slowly
I drifted backwards in the power of the constant flow which
washes away with the patience of eternity the immobile rocks.
The walls of the gorge are the layered history of the encounter
between the static rocks of a mountain range and the force of the
river carving its way to the sea.

About twenty thousand years ago, a massive flood tore
through the river channel to sculpt the main configurations of
the gorge as it exists today. A two thousand-foot-high ice dam
had blocked the flow of the river behind, and the impounded
waters backed up as far inland as the present state of Montana.
This lake covered an area of some three thousand square miles
and contained half the water volume of Lake Michigan. With
temperatures warming at the close of the ice age, the water broke
through the barrier and, in a massive release of water, swept
down the river channel in a flood that crested at twelve hundred
feet in Walulla Gap at the head of the gorge. Spilling out of the

west end of the gorge, the flood waters overflowed the Willamette River and flooded its valley as far south as Eugene. The Portland area was covered with four hundred feet of water. I was unable to comprehend such a cataclysmic event, but the record was there for me to see in the walls of the gorge as I journeyed upstream on the river that had formed it.

Another story revealed in the wall of the gorge was the history of transportation routes built through the river corridor. Railroad tracks parallel both river shores, successors to the first tracks pushed through the gorge in the 1880s. In 1913, Sam Hill began construction of the first highway through the river gorge. Outside of Europe, there were no roads like it, and the highway – with its dry, masonry stonework of bridges, tunnels, and retaining walls – was an engineering and aesthetic marvel when it opened in 1915.

Passing beneath Crown Point, I could see a section of the highway looping downward from Crown Point in terraced turns to the level of the river. There is a harmony between this old road and the slope it descends, a unity of the curve of road with the contour of hill.

By contrast, the modern freeway skirts cliffside and river edge with linear disdain. It paves its own way through the gorge, river and rock be damned. The two roadways stand in contrast: the old road plays with the hill in serpentine turns, almost reluctant to reach the bottom. The new highway, without elevation or curve, is just anxious to get through.

Beacon Rock, 141 miles inland from the mouth of the Columbia, stands at the head of the tide on the river. The effect is negligible, but was enough to be noted with relief by Lewis and Clark on the morning of 2 November 1805, as they descended the last rapids of the Columbia River.

I went ashore at Beacon Rock and climbed the zig-zag stairway built by Portlander Henry Biddle in 1918. From its 840-foot summit, I looked upriver to the barrier of Bonneville Dam which marked the end of my journey on the Columbia. Like Broughton, my voyage was an exploration of the river inland along its maritime reach of the sea, and it ended at the point where the land expedition of Lewis and Clark arrived at that sea-connected river.

For nearly 150 miles, I had followed along the unchanged water level of that shoreline visiting the sites of old Indian villages, the camps of the Lewis and Clark expedition, the rotting piers of early river communities, and the islands of the lower river. Behind Bonneville Dam, the old Columbia is no more. Only 146 years separate the discovery of the river from its drowning with the construction of the Bonneville Dam. All history, Indian and white, and the old River of the West, now lies under the waters of its impounded lake.

Bibliography

Amos, William H. *The Infinite River*. New York: 1970.

Appelo, Carlton E. *The Altoona Story: Wahkiatum County, Washington*. Deep Water, WA: 1972.

—. *The Cottardi Station Story: Wahkiatum County, Washington*. Deep Water, WA: 1980.

—. *Deep River—The C. Arthur Appelo Story*. Deep Water, WA: 1978.

—. *Frankfort on the Columbia*. Deep Water, WA: 1956.

—. *Knappton, The First 50 Years: Pacific County, Washington*. Deep River, WA: 1975.

—. *Pillar Rock: Wahkiakum County, Washington*. Deep River, WA: 1969.

Cathlamet Pioneer, the Paintings of Maude Kimball Butler. Notes by Julia Butler Hansen. Tacoma, WA: 1973.

Cobbe, Hugh. *Cook's Voyages and People of the Pacific*. London: 1979.

Columbia River Estuary Study Task Force. *Columbia River Estuary Inventory*. Astoria, OR: 1977.

Corning, Howard McKinley. *Dictionary of Oregon History*. Portland: 1956.

Gough, Barry M. *The Royal Navy and the Northwest Coast of North America, 1810–1914: A Study of British Maritime Ascendancy*. Vancouver, British Columbia: 1971.

Hezeta, Bruno de. *For Honor and Country: The Diary of Bruno de Hezeta*. Translated and annotated by Herbert K. Beals. Portland: 1985.

Holbrook, Stewart. *The Columbia*. New York: 1974.

Irving, Washington. *Astoria*. Edited by Edgeley W. Todd. Norman, OK: 1964.

Johansen, Dorothy O., and Charles M. Gate. *Empire of the Columbia: A History of the Northwest*. New York: 1957.

Lewis, Meriwether, and William Clark. *Journals of Lewis and Clark*. Edited by Bernard DeVoto. Boston: 1953.

Lewis, Meriwether, and William Clark. *Original Journals of the Lewis and Clark Expedition*, Vol. 3, Edited by Reuben Gold Thwaites. New York: 1959.

Lockley, Fred. *History of the Columbia River Valley*. Indianapolis: 1928.

McArthur, Lewis A. *Oregon Geographic Names*, 5th ed. Portland: 1982.

McClelland, John M. Jr. *Longview, The Remarkable Beginnings of a Modern Western City*. Portland: 1966.

Metcalfe, Philip, and Gene Itzen. *Bar Guide of the North Pacific Coast*. Astoria, OR: 1976.

Miller, Emma Gene. *Clatsop County, Oregon*. Portland: 1958.

Pacific Northwest River Basins Commission. *Columbia's Gateway, A History of the Columbia River Estuary to 1920*. Vancouver, WA: 1980.

Richmond, Henry R. *The History of the Portland District Corps of Engineers, 1871–1969*. Portland: 1970.

Ruby, Robert H., and John A. Brown. *Ferry Boats on the Columbia River*. Seattle: 1974.

Smith, Courtland I. *Salmon Fishers of the Columbia*. Corvallis, OR: 1976.

United States National Ocean Survey. *United States Coast Pilot*, Vol. 7. Washington, D.C.: 1978.

Wayburn, Peggy. *Edge of Life*. San Francisco: 1972.

Colophon

ALL TEXT AND DISPLAY copy in *Reach of Tide, Ring of History* is set in the photocomposition version of Bembo. The original Bembo was designed by Francesco Griffo for Aldus Manutius' publication of Pietro Cardinal Bembo's *De Aetna* (1496). Often considered the first of the "Old Faces," Bembo was the forerunner of the standard European typestyles used over the next two centuries. The capitals are shorter than the ascending lower case letters, and the T has divergent serifs.

Reach of Tide, Ring of History is printed on 70 lb. Warren Olde Style, an acid-free paper conforming to national permanent paper standards. The three-piece, combination binding consists of Holliston Mills Payko and Vellum finish James River Graphics Papan.

The production of this volume was accomplished through the skills and cooperation of the following:

Typesetting: Harrison Typesetting, Inc.
Paper: Zellerbach Paper Company
Printing: Artline Printers & Lithographers
Binding: Lincoln & Allen Company

LONG BEACH PENINSULA

Willapa Bay

WASHINGTON

● CATHLAMET

● ASTORIA

Columbia River

OREGON

Pacific Ocean

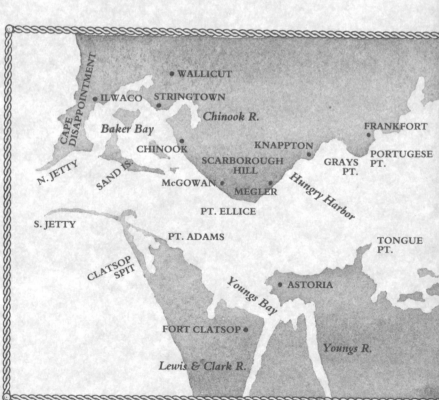

● WALLICUT

CAPE DISAPPOINTMENT

● ILWACO   STRINGTOWN

Chinook R.

FRANKFORT

Baker Bay

KNAPPTON

PORTUGESE PT.

CHINOOK

SCARBOROUGH HILL

GRAYS PT.

N. JETTY

SAND IS.

McGOWAN   MEGLER

Hungry Harbor

PT. ELLICE

S. JETTY

PT. ADAMS

TONGUE PT.

CLATSOP SPIT

Youngs Bay   ● ASTORIA

FORT CLATSOP ●

Youngs R.

Lewis & Clark R.